THE JEWISH ROOTS OF MARY

A Different Look at the Iconic Hebrew Woman

Dr. Maxwell Shimba

Shimba Publishing, LLC.

SHIMBA
PUBLISHING

TABLE OF CONTENTS

Introduction..vi

Chapter 01...1

Mary in the Hebrew Scriptures....................................1

Chapter 02...7

Mary's Jewish Heritage and Lineage..........................7

Chapter 03...13

Mary in Second Temple Judaism 13

Chapter 04...20

Mary and the Messianic Prophecies 20

Chapter 05...28

Mary's Role in God's Redemptive Plan 28

Chapter 06...36

Mary as the New Eve..36

Chapter 07...44

Mary as the New Queen Mother 44

Chapter 08...51

Mary as the New Ark of the Covenant........................51

Chapter 09...59

Mary as the Woman Clothed with the Sun 59

Chapter 10...66

Mary in the Early Christin Writings............................66

Chapter 11...73

The Evolution of Marian Theology in the Church 73

Chapter 12...81

Mary in Catholic Theology 81

Chapter 13...88

Mary in Protestant Theology 88

Chapter 14... 96

Mary and Intercessory Prayer.. 96

Chapter 15.. 104

Bringing the Divide: A Balanced Perspective on Mary............... 104

Chapter 16.. 111

Embracing The Fullness of Mary's Legacy 111

Appendices.. 117

INTRODUCTION

Rediscovering Mary

Mary, the Mother of Jesus, is one of the most revered figures in Christianity. Her significance spans Catholic and Protestant traditions, yet the way she is perceived and honored varies significantly between these two branches of Christianity. Catholics hold Mary in high esteem, venerating her as the Mother of God and intercessor, while Protestants often emphasize her role as a humble servant of God, focusing more on her humanity and less on her divine significance. These divergent views have led to a complex and sometimes contentious relationship with Mary within the broader Christian community. This book aims to rediscover Mary by examining her Jewish roots and presenting a balanced perspective that honors her role in God's redemptive plan.

The Catholic View of Mary

In Catholic theology, Mary holds a place of unique honor. She is often referred to as the "New Eve," the "Queen of Heaven," and the "Mother of the Church." Catholic doctrine includes beliefs in her Immaculate Conception, perpetual virginity, and Assumption into heaven. Catholics also believe in Mary's intercessory power, praying to her to intercede on their behalf with her son, Jesus. This veneration of Mary is deeply rooted in Catholic tradition and liturgy, reflecting a profound respect for her role in salvation history.

The Protestant View of Mary

Protestants, on the other hand, generally hold a different view. While recognizing Mary as the mother of Jesus and honoring her obedience and faithfulness, Protestants do not accord her the same level of veneration seen in Catholicism. The Reformation brought about a focus on sola scriptura (scripture alone), leading to a rejection of many traditions and practices not explicitly found in the Bible. As a result, Protestant theology tends to emphasize Mary's humanity and her role as a model of faith and obedience, rather than as a divine intercessor.

The Need for Reevaluation

The stark differences in how Mary is viewed within Catholic and Protestant traditions highlight the need for a reevaluation of her role and significance. Both perspectives offer valuable insights but can also be seen as incomplete. Catholics may elevate Mary to a status that seems almost divine, potentially overshadowing the singular role of Christ in salvation. Protestants, conversely, might miss the depth of Mary's significance in God's plan by focusing too narrowly on her humanity. To bridge this divide, it is essential to revisit the historical and cultural context of Mary's life, particularly her Jewish roots.

Mary's Jewish Heritage

Mary was a Jewish woman living in first-century Palestine. Her Jewish identity is often overlooked in Christian theology, yet it is crucial for understanding her role and significance. The Jewish traditions, scriptures, and expectations of the Messiah deeply influenced Mary's life and actions. By exploring her Jewish heritage, we can gain a richer and more nuanced understanding of Mary. This approach allows us to see Mary not just as the Mother of Jesus, but as a faithful Jewish woman who played a pivotal role in the fulfillment of God's promises to Israel.

A Balanced Perspective

This book aims to present a balanced perspective on Mary, one that honors her Jewish roots and acknowledges her significant role in God's redemptive plan. We will explore key questions about Mary's identity and role, such as: Can Mary really pray for us? Is Mary truly the New Eve, the New Queen Mother, the New Ark, and the Woman Clothed with the Sun? By examining these questions through the lens of both Catholic and Protestant traditions, and grounding our exploration in Mary's Jewish heritage, we hope to provide a more comprehensive and unified understanding of this iconic Hebrew woman.

Moving Forward

As we embark on this journey of rediscovery, we invite readers to set aside preconceived notions and open their hearts and minds to a deeper understanding of Mary. By reevaluating her role and significance, we can appreciate the richness of her legacy and her profound impact on the Christian faith. Mary's story is not just a tale of a young woman chosen by God; it is a story of faith, obedience, and divine purpose that transcends denominational boundaries. Through this exploration, we hope to honor Mary in a way that unites rather than divides, offering a holistic view that reflects the fullness of her legacy.

This introduction sets the stage for a comprehensive and balanced exploration of Mary, rooted in her Jewish heritage and examining her significance in both Catholic and Protestant traditions. The goal is to bridge the divide and offer a richer, more nuanced understanding of Mary, the iconic Hebrew woman who played a pivotal role in God's redemptive plan.

DR. MAXWELL SHIMBA

CHAPTER 01

MARY IN THE HEBREW SCRIPTURES

Mary, the Mother of Jesus, holds a significant place in Christian theology, but her story does not begin in the New Testament. To fully appreciate her role, we must turn our attention to the Hebrew Scriptures, where we find subtle yet powerful anticipations of Mary. This chapter will explore the Old Testament references and foreshadowings that point to Mary, examining their theological implications and how they lay the groundwork for her unique role in salvation history.

The Protoevangelium: Genesis 3:15

One of the earliest and most significant references to Mary in the Hebrew Scriptures is found in Genesis 3:15, often referred to as the Protoevangelium or "First Gospel." This verse occurs immediately after the Fall of Adam and Eve, when God pronounces a curse upon the serpent:

"I will put enmity between you and the woman and between your offspring and her offspring; he shall bruise your head, and you shall bruise his heel" (Genesis 3:15, ESV).

Traditionally, Christians have interpreted this passage as a prophecy concerning the Messiah and His mother. The "woman" is seen as a foreshadowing of Mary, and her "offspring" is understood to be Jesus Christ. This enmity between the serpent and the woman, and the ultimate victory of her offspring, suggests a special, divinely appointed role for Mary in the redemption of humanity.

The Ark of the Covenant: A Foreshadowing of Mary

Another profound typological foreshadowing of Mary is found in the Ark of the Covenant. The Ark, which held the tablets of the Law, a jar of manna, and Aaron's rod, represented God's presence among His people. The parallels between the Ark and Mary are striking:

- Presence of God: Just as the Ark carried the presence of God in the Old Testament, Mary bore the Son of God in her womb.

- Holy and Untouched: The Ark was made of acacia wood and overlaid with gold, symbolizing its purity and sanctity. Similarly, Mary is often referred to as "full of grace" (Luke 1:28) and venerated for her purity.

- Bearer of the Covenant: The Ark carried the Old Covenant (the Law), while Mary carried the New Covenant (Jesus Christ) within her.

This typology is further supported by the account of the Visitation in Luke 1:39-56. Mary's visit to Elizabeth echoes the journey of the Ark to the house of Obed-edom in 2 Samuel 6:1-11. Both accounts describe a joyous response to the presence of God: John the Baptist leaps in Elizabeth's womb, and David dances before the Ark.

The Queen Mother: 1 Kings 2:19

In ancient Israel, the queen's mother held a position of great honor and influence. One notable example is Bathsheba, the mother of King Solomon. In 1 Kings 2:19, we read:

"So Bathsheba went to King Solomon to speak to him on behalf of Adonijah. And the king rose to meet her and bowed down to her. Then he sat on his throne and had a seat brought for the king's mother, and she sat on his right."

This practice of honoring the queen mother (gebirah) is seen as a foreshadowing of Mary's role as the Queen of

Heaven. Just as Bathsheba interceded on behalf of Adonijah, Mary is believed to intercede for believers, a role acknowledged in Catholic theology.

The Virgin Birth: Isaiah 7:14

The prophecy of Isaiah 7:14 is one of the clearest Old Testament references to Mary:

"Therefore the Lord himself will give you a sign. Behold, the virgin shall conceive and bear a son, and shall call his name Immanuel" (Isaiah 7:14, ESV).

This prophecy is directly quoted in Matthew 1:23, identifying Mary as the virgin who gives birth to Jesus, Immanuel ("God with us"). The fulfillment of this prophecy underscores Mary's unique role in salvation history and her divine selection to be the mother of the Messiah.

The Suffering Servant's Mother: Isaiah 53

While Isaiah 53 is primarily known for its vivid depiction of the Suffering Servant, many theologians see an implicit reference to Mary in the background. The Suffering Servant's mother, who witnesses her son's pain and suffering, can be seen as a foreshadowing of Mary standing at the foot of the cross (John 19:25-27). Her silent presence in the prophecy reflects her profound participation in her son's mission and suffering.

Hannah and Mary: 1 Samuel 1-2

Hannah, the mother of Samuel, offers another typological parallel to Mary. Hannah's song of praise in 1 Samuel 2:1-10 closely resembles Mary's Magnificat in Luke 1:46-55. Both songs celebrate God's intervention and mercy, highlighting themes of divine reversal and salvation:

- Hannah's Prayer: "My heart exults in the Lord; my strength is exalted in the Lord... He raises up the poor from the dust; he lifts the needy from the ash heap to make them sit with princes and inherit a seat of honor" (1 Samuel 2:1, 8, ESV).

- Mary's Magnificat: "My soul magnifies the Lord, and my spirit rejoices in God my Savior... He has brought down the mighty from their thrones and exalted those of humble estate; he has filled the hungry with good things, and the rich he has sent away empty" (Luke 1:46-47, 52-53, ESV).

The parallels between Hannah and Mary emphasize God's faithfulness and the continuity of His redemptive work across generations.

Esther: The Intercessor

The story of Esther provides another powerful foreshadowing of Mary's role as an intercessor. Esther, a Jewish queen, courageously intercedes for her people, risking her life to save them from destruction (Esther 4:16). In a similar vein, Mary is seen as an intercessor for the faithful, advocating on their behalf before her son, Jesus. The bravery and advocacy of Esther prefigure Mary's spiritual intercession.

Conclusion: The Foundation of Mary's Role

The Hebrew Scriptures lay a rich foundation for understanding Mary's role in salvation history. Through typological foreshadowings and prophetic references, we see glimpses of her significance long before her appearance in the New Testament. From the Protoevangelium in Genesis to the intercessory role of Esther, these Old Testament texts illuminate Mary's unique place in God's plan, preparing the way for her pivotal role as the Mother of the Messiah.

By appreciating these foreshadowings, we gain a deeper understanding of Mary's significance, not only in Christian theology but also in the broader narrative of God's redemptive work. This perspective allows us to honor Mary in a way that is faithful to her Jewish heritage and her unparalleled contribution to the story of salvation.

CHAPTER 02

MARY'S JEWISH HERITAGE AND LINEAGE

Mary, the mother of Jesus, occupies a central role in Christian theology, but to fully understand her significance, it is essential to explore her Jewish heritage and lineage. This chapter will delve into Mary's family background, her descent from the House of David, and her place within the Jewish community of her time.

Mary's Family Background

The Gospels provide some details about Mary's family, although much of her early life remains shrouded in mystery. According to tradition, Mary's parents were Joachim and Anne, devout Jews who dedicated their daughter to the service of God. While these details are not found in the canonical Gospels, they are preserved in apocryphal writings such as the Protoevangelium of James, which provides a glimpse into the pious and faithful environment in which Mary was raised.

Lineage from the House of David

One of the most significant aspects of Mary's heritage is her descent from the House of David. This lineage is crucial because it fulfills Old Testament prophecies regarding the Messiah's ancestry. The prophet Nathan conveyed God's promise to David, saying, "Your house and your kingdom shall be made sure forever before me. Your throne shall be established forever" (2 Samuel 7:16, ESV). This Davidic covenant established that the Messiah would come from David's lineage.

The Gospel of Matthew provides a genealogy that traces Jesus' lineage through Joseph, establishing a legal claim to the Davidic line. While Joseph is not Jesus' biological father, his marriage to Mary legally places Jesus within David's lineage. Matthew 1:16 states, "And Jacob the father of Joseph, the husband of Mary, of whom Jesus was born, who is called Christ" (ESV).

Luke's Gospel offers another genealogy, which many scholars believe traces Mary's lineage, although it is recorded in Joseph's name, following Jewish custom. Luke 3:23-38 presents a different genealogical path that also leads back to David, suggesting that Mary herself was a descendant of David. This dual genealogical record reinforces Jesus' legitimate claim to the Davidic throne from both a legal and a biological standpoint.

Mary in the Jewish Community

Mary lived in Nazareth, a small town in Galilee, during a time of significant political and social upheaval. The Jewish people were under Roman occupation, and there was a widespread longing for the Messiah who would liberate them and restore the kingdom of Israel. Mary's Jewish identity was deeply rooted in this context of expectation and hope.

As a young Jewish woman, Mary would have been raised in the traditions and customs of her faith. She would have observed the Sabbath, participated in synagogue worship, and adhered to the dietary laws outlined in the Torah. Her life would have been steeped in the stories and prophecies of the Hebrew Scriptures, including those that foretold the coming of the Messiah.

Betrothal and Marriage Customs

Mary's betrothal to Joseph reflects the Jewish customs of her time. Betrothal was a formal engagement, more binding than modern-day engagements, and could only be broken by a formal divorce. During the betrothal period, the couple was considered legally married, although they did not live together or consummate the marriage until after the wedding ceremony.

Mary's acceptance of the angel Gabriel's message, announcing that she would conceive by the Holy Spirit, demonstrates her profound faith and obedience. This announcement, known as the Annunciation, is recorded in Luke 1:26-38. Mary's response, "Behold, I am the servant of the Lord; let it be to me according to your word" (Luke 1:38, ESV), reflects her deep trust in God and her willingness to embrace her role in His plan, despite the personal risks and social implications.

The Significance of Mary's Jewish Heritage

Understanding Mary's Jewish heritage is crucial for several reasons. First, it situates her within the broader narrative of God's covenantal relationship with Israel. Mary's life and role cannot be fully appreciated without recognizing her place within this unfolding story of redemption that spans from the call of Abraham to the coming of the Messiah.

Second, Mary's Jewish heritage highlights the fulfillment of Old Testament prophecies and promises. Her descent from David connects Jesus to the Davidic covenant, affirming His identity as the promised Messiah. This connection is vital for both Jewish and Christian theological frameworks, as it underscores the continuity between the Old and New Testaments.

Third, Mary's Jewish identity enriches our understanding of her faith and character. Her piety, courage, and obedience are rooted in the traditions and teachings of her people. Recognizing Mary as a faithful Jewish woman allows us to appreciate her unique role in God's plan and the profound faith that she exemplified.

Conclusion: Embracing Mary's Heritage

Mary's Jewish heritage and lineage provide a deeper and more nuanced understanding of her role in salvation history. Her descent from the House of David, her upbringing in a devout Jewish family, and her faithful adherence to the traditions of her people all contribute to her unique place in God's plan.

By exploring Mary's Jewish roots, we gain a richer appreciation for her significance and the fulfillment of God's promises through her. This perspective not only honors Mary's heritage but also bridges the gap between the Old and

New Testaments, highlighting the continuity of God's redemptive work across the ages.

As we continue to delve into Mary's story, let us keep in mind her profound connection to the Jewish faith and the rich tapestry of history and prophecy that surrounds her. In doing so, we can honor her legacy and better understand the pivotal role she plays in the narrative of God's salvation for humanity.

CHAPTER 03

MARY IN SECOND TEMPLE JUDAISM

To fully appreciate Mary's life and faith, it is essential to understand the religious and cultural context of Second Temple Judaism, the period in which she lived. This era, spanning from the rebuilding of the Jerusalem Temple in 516 BCE to its destruction in 70 CE, was marked by significant religious, social, and political developments. This chapter will provide insights into the beliefs and practices of Second Temple Judaism, highlighting how these shaped Mary's worldview and her pivotal role in salvation history.

The Historical Context of Second Temple Judaism

Second Temple Judaism was a dynamic period characterized by a diverse range of religious expressions and expectations. Following the Babylonian exile, the Jewish community returned to Jerusalem and rebuilt the Temple, which became the center of religious life. During this time, several key developments occurred:

1. Hellenistic Influence: The conquests of Alexander the Great brought Greek culture and language to the region, leading to the Hellenization of many aspects of Jewish life. This influence is evident in the widespread use of the Greek language (e.g., the Septuagint, a Greek translation of the Hebrew Scriptures) and the adoption of certain Hellenistic customs and ideas.

2. The Hasmonean Dynasty: Following the Maccabean Revolt (167-160 BCE), the Hasmonean dynasty established an independent Jewish kingdom. This period saw a resurgence of Jewish nationalism and religious fervor, as well as conflicts between different Jewish sects.

3. Roman Occupation: In 63 BCE, Pompey the Great conquered Jerusalem, bringing Judea under Roman rule. Roman occupation introduced new political dynamics and tensions, contributing to the Jewish expectation of a Messiah who would liberate them from foreign domination.

Religious Beliefs and Practices

The religious landscape of Second Temple Judaism was rich and varied, with several key beliefs and practices shaping the community's faith and identity:

1. Monotheism: The belief in one God, Yahweh, was central to Jewish identity. This monotheism was expressed through worship, prayer, and the study of the Torah. The Shema, a declaration of God's oneness, was recited daily: "Hear, O Israel: The Lord our God, the Lord is one" (Deuteronomy 6:4, ESV).

2. The Temple: The Second Temple in Jerusalem was the focal point of Jewish worship. It was here that sacrifices were offered, festivals celebrated, and prayers lifted. Pilgrimage to the Temple during major festivals such as Passover, Shavuot, and Sukkot was an essential aspect of Jewish religious life.

3. The Torah: The Torah (the first five books of the Hebrew Scriptures) was the foundation of Jewish law and practice. It guided daily life, ethical conduct, and religious observance. The study and interpretation of the Torah were central to Jewish education and piety.

4. Messianic Expectation: The hope for a Messiah, a divinely anointed leader who would restore Israel and establish God's kingdom, was a prominent feature of Second

Temple Judaism. This expectation was fueled by prophecies in the Hebrew Scriptures, such as those found in Isaiah, Jeremiah, and Daniel.

5. Synagogue Worship: In addition to the Temple, local synagogues served as centers for worship, teaching, and community life. Synagogue services included the reading of the Torah, prayers, and instruction in the Scriptures.

Jewish Sects and Movements

Second Temple Judaism was not monolithic; it included various sects and movements, each with its own beliefs and practices:

1. Pharisees: The Pharisees emphasized strict adherence to the Torah and the oral traditions. They believed in the resurrection of the dead, angels, and an afterlife. The Pharisees were influential in shaping Jewish thought and practice, particularly in the development of Rabbinic Judaism.

2. Sadducees: The Sadducees were a priestly aristocratic group that controlled the Temple and its rituals. They rejected the oral traditions upheld by the Pharisees and did not believe in the resurrection or an afterlife. Their authority waned after the destruction of the Temple.

3. Essenes: The Essenes were a separatist group that lived in communal settlements, most famously at Qumran near the Dead Sea. They emphasized purity, apocalyptic

expectations, and a strict adherence to the law. The Dead Sea Scrolls, discovered in the 20th century, are attributed to this group.

4. Zealots: The Zealots were a revolutionary group that sought to overthrow Roman rule through armed resistance. Their fervent nationalism and militant actions culminated in the First Jewish-Roman War (66-70 CE), which led to the destruction of the Second Temple.

Mary's Place within This Context

Mary's life and faith were deeply influenced by the religious and cultural environment of Second Temple Judaism. Her Jewish identity shaped her beliefs, practices, and expectations, providing a framework for understanding her response to God's call.

1. Devout Faith: As a devout Jew, Mary would have participated in the religious practices of her community, including synagogue worship, prayer, and the observance of Jewish festivals. Her familiarity with the Hebrew Scriptures is evident in her Magnificat (Luke 1:46-55), which echoes themes and phrases from the Psalms and the song of Hannah.

2. Messianic Hope: Mary's acceptance of the angel Gabriel's message (Luke 1:26-38) must be understood in light of the messianic expectations of her time. The promise that her son would be called "the Son of the Most High" and

would "reign over the house of Jacob forever" (Luke 1:32-33, ESV) resonated with the hope for a divinely anointed king who would fulfill God's promises to Israel.

3. Role of Women: While women's roles in Second Temple Judaism were generally more private and domestic, they were nonetheless significant. Women like Mary were expected to uphold the religious and cultural traditions of their households, ensuring the transmission of faith to the next generation. Mary's prominence in the Gospels highlights her extraordinary faith and obedience within this context.

4. Purity and Piety: The emphasis on ritual purity and piety in Second Temple Judaism is reflected in Mary's life. Her response to Gabriel, "Behold, I am the servant of the Lord; let it be to me according to your word" (Luke 1:38, ESV), demonstrates her deep commitment to God's will and her readiness to fulfill her divinely appointed role.

Conclusion: Mary in Her Context

Understanding the religious and cultural context of Second Temple Judaism is crucial for appreciating Mary's life and faith. Her devout adherence to Jewish practices, her messianic hope, and her remarkable response to God's call are all rooted in the rich traditions and expectations of her time.

By situating Mary within this historical and religious framework, we gain a deeper insight into her significance and the extraordinary nature of her role in God's redemptive plan. Mary was not only a young Jewish woman chosen by God but also a pivotal figure whose faith and obedience resonate within the broader narrative of Second Temple Judaism and its profound impact on the unfolding story of salvation.

As we continue to explore Mary's story, let us keep in mind the vibrant and diverse context of Second Temple Judaism, which shaped her faith and identity. In doing so, we can better appreciate the depth of her legacy and her unique contribution to the Christian faith.

CHAPTER 04

MARY AND THE MESSIANIC PROPHECIES

The Messianic prophecies in the Old Testament form a vital part of the Jewish anticipation for a future anointed leader who would redeem and restore Israel. Mary, as the mother of Jesus, is intricately linked to these prophecies, fulfilling key aspects that highlight her unique role in salvation history. This chapter will analyze several major Messianic prophecies and examine how Mary's life and actions fulfill these ancient promises.

The Virgin Birth: Isaiah 7:14

One of the most prominent Messianic prophecies is found in Isaiah 7:14:

"Therefore the Lord himself will give you a sign. Behold, the virgin shall conceive and bear a son, and shall call his name Immanuel" (Isaiah 7:14, ESV).

This prophecy, given by the prophet Isaiah to King Ahaz of Judah, promised a sign of divine intervention: a virgin would conceive and give birth to a child named Immanuel, meaning "God with us." The Gospel of Matthew explicitly links this prophecy to Mary and the birth of Jesus:

"All this took place to fulfill what the Lord had spoken by the prophet: 'Behold, the virgin shall conceive and bear a son, and they shall call his name Immanuel' (which means, God with us)" (Matthew 1:22-23, ESV).

Mary's virginal conception, as announced by the angel Gabriel, fulfills this ancient prophecy, affirming her unique role as the mother of the Messiah who embodies God's presence among His people.

The Seed of the Woman: Genesis 3:15

The Protoevangelium, or "First Gospel," found in Genesis 3:15, is another key Messianic prophecy:

"I will put enmity between you and the woman, and between your offspring and her offspring; he shall bruise your head, and you shall bruise his heel" (Genesis 3:15, ESV).

This verse, spoken by God after the fall of Adam and Eve, foretells the ongoing struggle between the serpent (Satan) and the offspring of the woman. The promise of a future offspring who would crush the serpent's head is seen as a foreshadowing of the Messiah's victory over sin and evil. Mary, as the mother of Jesus, plays a crucial role in this prophecy. Her son, Jesus, is the promised offspring who defeats Satan through His death and resurrection. Thus, Mary's motherhood is integral to the fulfillment of this ancient promise.

The Davidic Covenant: 2 Samuel 7:12-16

The Davidic Covenant, articulated in 2 Samuel 7:12-16, is central to the Messianic expectations of the Old Testament:

"When your days are fulfilled and you lie down with your fathers, I will raise up your offspring after you, who shall come from your body, and I will establish his kingdom. He shall build a house for my name, and I will establish the throne of his kingdom forever" (2 Samuel 7:12-13, ESV).

This covenant, made with King David, promised that his descendants would rule an everlasting kingdom. The prophets further elaborated on this promise, describing a future Davidic king who would bring justice and peace. Mary, a descendant of David (as established in both Matthew and Luke's genealogies), fulfills this prophecy through her son, Jesus, who is proclaimed as the Son of David and the rightful heir to David's throne. The angel Gabriel's announcement to Mary highlights this connection:

"He will be great and will be called the Son of the Most High. And the Lord God will give to him the throne of his father David, and he will reign over the house of Jacob forever, and of his kingdom there will be no end" (Luke 1:32-33, ESV).

The Suffering Servant: Isaiah 53

Isaiah 53 provides a profound and detailed description of the Suffering Servant, a figure who bears the sins of the people and brings redemption through his suffering and death:

"But he was pierced for our transgressions; he was crushed for our iniquities; upon him was the chastisement that brought us peace, and with his wounds we are healed" (Isaiah 53:5, ESV).

While this prophecy primarily focuses on the Messiah's sacrificial role, Mary's participation in her son's mission is also significant. Mary's presence at the foot of the cross, witnessing Jesus' suffering and death, underscores her deep connection to the Suffering Servant's mission. Her willingness to endure this agony, as foretold by Simeon in Luke 2:35 ("and a sword will pierce through your own soul also"), reflects her integral role in the fulfillment of this prophecy.

The Birthplace of the Messiah: Micah 5:2

The prophet Micah foretold the birthplace of the Messiah in Bethlehem:

"But you, O Bethlehem Ephrathah, who are too little to be among the clans of Judah, from you shall come forth for me one who is to be ruler in Israel, whose coming forth is from of old, from ancient days" (Micah 5:2, ESV).

This prophecy is fulfilled through Mary, who gives birth to Jesus in Bethlehem, as recorded in the Gospel of Luke:

"And Joseph also went up from Galilee, from the town of Nazareth, to Judea, to the city of David, which is called Bethlehem, because he was of the house and lineage of David, to be registered with Mary, his betrothed, who was with child. And while they were there, the time came for her to give birth. And she gave birth to her firstborn son and wrapped him in swaddling cloths and laid him in a manger" (Luke 2:4-7, ESV).

Mary's journey to Bethlehem and the birth of Jesus there directly fulfill Micah's prophecy, highlighting her crucial role in bringing the Messiah into the world.

The New Covenant: Jeremiah 31:31-34

Jeremiah prophesied about a new covenant that God would establish with His people:

"Behold, the days are coming, declares the Lord, when I will make a new covenant with the house of Israel and the house of Judah... For this is the covenant that I will make with the house of Israel after those days, declares the Lord: I will put my law within them, and I will write it on their hearts. And I will be their God, and they shall be my people" (Jeremiah 31:31, 33, ESV).

Jesus, through His life, death, and resurrection, inaugurates this new covenant. Mary, as the mother of Jesus, is intimately connected to this fulfillment. Her acceptance of God's will and her role in the Incarnation make her a pivotal figure in the establishment of the new covenant. The angel Gabriel's message to Mary signifies the beginning of this transformative covenantal relationship.

The Return of Elijah: Malachi 4:5-6

The prophet Malachi foretold the return of Elijah before the coming of the great and dreadful day of the Lord:

"Behold, I will send you Elijah the prophet before the great and awesome day of the Lord comes. And he will turn the hearts of fathers to their children and the hearts of children to their fathers, lest I come and strike the land with a decree of utter destruction" (Malachi 4:5-6, ESV).

This prophecy is fulfilled in the ministry of John the Baptist, who comes in the spirit and power of Elijah (Luke 1:17) to prepare the way for the Lord. Mary's connection to this prophecy is through her relative Elizabeth, the mother of John the Baptist. The visit of Mary to Elizabeth, where John leaps in the womb at the sound of Mary's greeting (Luke 1:39-45), signifies the close relationship between Mary and the fulfillment of Malachi's prophecy through John.

Conclusion: Mary's Fulfillment of Messianic Prophecies

Mary's life and role are deeply intertwined with the fulfillment of Messianic prophecies in the Old Testament. Her virgin birth fulfills Isaiah's prophecy, her descent from David fulfills the Davidic Covenant, and her giving birth to Jesus in Bethlehem fulfills Micah's prophecy. Furthermore, her participation in Jesus' mission and suffering aligns with the Suffering Servant of Isaiah, and her connection to the new covenant reflects Jeremiah's prophecy.

By examining these prophecies and their fulfillment in Mary, we gain a richer understanding of her unique role in God's redemptive plan. Mary is not only the mother of Jesus but also a pivotal figure through whom the ancient promises of God are realized. Her life exemplifies faith, obedience, and profound connection to the divine narrative that spans the Hebrew Scriptures and the New Testament. Through Mary, we see the continuity of God's promises and their ultimate fulfillment in the Messiah, Jesus Christ.

CHAPTER 05

MARY'S ROLE IN GOD'S REDEMPTIVE PLAN

Mary, the mother of Jesus, occupies a unique and pivotal position in God's redemptive plan. Her role in the Incarnation and her extraordinary faith and obedience have profound implications for salvation history. This chapter will explore Mary's significance in God's plan for redemption, examining biblical evidence and insights from exhaustive concordances and comprehensive commentaries.

The Annunciation: The Beginning of the Incarnation

The Annunciation, recorded in Luke 1:26-38, marks the moment when God's redemptive plan began to take tangible form through Mary. The angel Gabriel appeared to Mary with a message that would change the course of history:

"In the sixth month the angel Gabriel was sent from God to a city of Galilee named Nazareth, to a virgin betrothed to a man whose name was Joseph, of the house of David. And the virgin's name was Mary. And he came to her and said, 'Greetings, O favored one, the Lord is with you!' But she was greatly troubled at the saying, and tried to discern what sort of greeting this might be. And the angel said to her, 'Do not be afraid, Mary, for you have found favor with God. And behold, you will conceive in your womb and bear a son, and you shall call his name Jesus. He will be great and will be called the Son of the Most High. And the Lord God will give to him the throne of his father David, and he will reign over the house of Jacob forever, and of his kingdom there will be no end'" (Luke 1:26-33, ESV).

Gabriel's announcement highlights several key aspects of Mary's role:

1. Divine Favor: Mary is described as "favored" (Greek: κεχαριτωμένη, kecharitōmenē), indicating that she has been graced by God in a unique way.

2. Messianic Fulfillment: The promise that her son will inherit David's throne and reign forever directly connects Jesus to Messianic prophecies (2 Samuel 7:12-16).

Mary's response to Gabriel's message further underscores her role in God's redemptive plan:

"And Mary said, 'Behold, I am the servant of the Lord; let it be to me according to your word.' And the angel departed from her" (Luke 1:38, ESV).

Mary's willing acceptance of God's plan, despite the personal and social implications, demonstrates her profound faith and obedience. Her response exemplifies her role as a model disciple, fully trusting in God's word.

The Visitation: Proclamation and Confirmation

Following the Annunciation, Mary visits her relative Elizabeth, who is also miraculously pregnant with John the Baptist. This event, known as the Visitation, is recorded in Luke 1:39-45:

"In those days Mary arose and went with haste into the hill country, to a town in Judah, and she entered the house of Zechariah and greeted Elizabeth. And when Elizabeth heard the greeting of Mary, the baby leaped in her womb. And Elizabeth was filled with the Holy Spirit, and she exclaimed with a loud cry, 'Blessed are you among women, and blessed is the fruit of your womb! And why is this granted to me that the mother of my Lord should come to me? For behold, when the sound of your greeting came to my ears, the baby in my womb leaped for joy. And blessed is she who believed that there would be a fulfillment of what was spoken to her from the Lord'" (Luke 1:39-45, ESV).

Elizabeth's proclamation, inspired by the Holy Spirit, confirms Mary's unique role and the significance of her faith. Elizabeth's recognition of Mary as "the mother of my Lord" underscores the divine nature of Mary's child and the fulfillment of God's promises.

The Magnificat: Mary's Song of Praise

Mary's response to Elizabeth's greeting is the Magnificat, a song of praise that reflects her deep understanding of God's redemptive work:

"And Mary said, 'My soul magnifies the Lord, and my spirit rejoices in God my Savior, for he has looked on the humble estate of his servant. For behold, from now on all generations will call me blessed; for he who is mighty has done great things for me, and holy is his name. And his mercy is for those who fear him from generation to generation. He has shown strength with his arm; he has scattered the proud in the thoughts of their hearts; he has brought down the mighty from their thrones and exalted those of humble estate; he has filled the hungry with good things, and the rich he has sent away empty. He has helped his servant Israel, in remembrance of his mercy, as he spoke to our fathers, to Abraham and to his offspring forever'" (Luke 1:46-55, ESV).

The Magnificat is rich with Old Testament allusions and echoes themes from the Psalms and the Song of Hannah (1 Samuel 2:1-10). Mary's song highlights:

1. God's Faithfulness: Mary praises God for His faithfulness to His promises and His mercy to those who fear Him.

2. Divine Reversal: The Magnificat emphasizes God's power to reverse social and economic inequalities, exalting the humble and filling the hungry.

3. Covenant Fulfillment: Mary connects her experience to God's covenant with Abraham, highlighting the continuity of God's redemptive plan.

The Birth of Jesus: Fulfillment of Prophecy

The birth of Jesus, recorded in Matthew 1:18-25 and Luke 2:1-7, fulfills several Old Testament prophecies and underscores Mary's role in God's plan:

"Now the birth of Jesus Christ took place in this way. When his mother Mary had been betrothed to Joseph, before they came together she was found to be with child from the Holy Spirit. And her husband Joseph, being a just man and unwilling to put her to shame, resolved to divorce her quietly.

But as he considered these things, behold, an angel of the Lord appeared to him in a dream, saying, 'Joseph, son of David, do not fear to take Mary as your wife, for that which is conceived in her is from the Holy Spirit. She will bear a son, and you shall call his name Jesus, for he will save his people from their sins.' All this took place to fulfill what the Lord had spoken by the prophet: 'Behold, the virgin shall conceive and bear a son, and they shall call his name Immanuel' (which means, God with us)" (Matthew 1:18-23, ESV).

Mary's virginal conception and the birth of Jesus in Bethlehem fulfill Isaiah 7:14 and Micah 5:2, respectively. These fulfillments highlight Mary's role in bringing God's promises to fruition.

Mary at the Crucifixion: Sharing in Jesus' Suffering

Mary's presence at the crucifixion, recorded in John 19:25-27, underscores her participation in Jesus' redemptive suffering:

"But standing by the cross of Jesus were his mother and his mother's sister, Mary the wife of Clopas, and Mary Magdalene. When Jesus saw his mother and the disciple whom he loved standing nearby, he said to his mother, 'Woman, behold, your son!' Then he said to the disciple, 'Behold, your mother!' And from that hour the disciple took her to his own home" (John 19:25-27, ESV).

Mary's presence at the cross fulfills Simeon's prophecy that a sword would pierce her soul (Luke 2:35). Her participation in Jesus' suffering illustrates her deep connection to His redemptive mission and her unique role as a model of faith and discipleship.

The Assumption and Coronation: Tradition and Theology

While not explicitly recorded in the Bible, the traditions of the Assumption and Coronation of Mary have been affirmed by various church teachings. The Assumption, the belief that Mary was taken body and soul into heaven, reflects her unique holiness and her close association with Jesus. The Coronation, the belief that Mary is crowned as Queen of Heaven, underscores her exalted role in the heavenly realm. These traditions highlight the theological significance of Mary's life and her ongoing intercessory role for believers.

Conclusion: Mary's Pivotal Role in Redemption

Mary's role in God's redemptive plan is multifaceted and profound. Her obedience and faith at the Annunciation, her proclamation in the Magnificat, her presence at the birth and crucifixion of Jesus, and her veneration in Christian tradition all highlight her unique position in salvation history. Mary's life exemplifies the model disciple, one who fully trusts and cooperates with God's will, making her an integral part of the story of redemption.

By examining the biblical evidence and theological insights, we gain a deeper appreciation of Mary's pivotal role in God's plan. Her life and actions fulfill ancient prophecies and demonstrate the continuity of God's redemptive work from the Old Testament to the New. Through Mary, we see the unfolding of God's promises and the ultimate realization of His plan for humanity's salvation.

CHAPTER 06

MARY AS THE NEW EVE

The typological parallel between Eve and Mary is a profound theme in Christian theology, emphasizing how Mary, as the New Eve, brings a new beginning through her son, Jesus Christ. This chapter will explore this typology, examining biblical evidence, insights from exhaustive concordances, and comprehensive commentaries to understand how Mary fulfills this role in God's redemptive plan.

The Fall and the Promise: Genesis 3

The story of Eve in Genesis sets the stage for understanding Mary as the New Eve. Eve's disobedience leads to the fall of humanity, but God immediately promises redemption through her offspring:

"And the Lord God said to the serpent, 'Because you have done this, cursed are you above all livestock and above all beasts of the field; on your belly you shall go, and dust you shall eat all the days of your life. I will put enmity between you and the woman, and between your offspring and her offspring; he shall bruise your head, and you shall bruise his heel'" (Genesis 3:14-15, ESV).

This passage, known as the Protoevangelium or "First Gospel," contains the first hint of the Messiah's coming and the victory over sin and Satan. The "woman" in this prophecy has been traditionally understood to refer both to Eve and, in a fuller sense, to Mary, whose offspring (Jesus) will ultimately defeat Satan.

The New Testament Perspective

The New Testament presents Mary as the fulfillment of the promise in Genesis. Several key passages highlight the contrast and parallel between Eve and Mary.

The Annunciation: Luke 1:26-38

The Annunciation is a pivotal moment where Mary's obedience contrasts with Eve's disobedience:

"In the sixth month the angel Gabriel was sent from God to a city of Galilee named Nazareth, to a virgin betrothed to a man whose name was Joseph, of the house of David. And the virgin's name was Mary. And he came to her and said, 'Greetings, O favored one, the Lord is with you!' But she was greatly troubled at the saying, and tried to discern what sort of greeting this might be. And the angel said to her, 'Do not be afraid, Mary, for you have found favor with God. And behold, you will conceive in your womb and bear a son, and you shall call his name Jesus. He will be great and will be called the Son of the Most High. And the Lord God will give to him the throne of his father David, and he will reign over the house of Jacob forever, and of his kingdom there will be no end.' And Mary said to the angel, 'How will this be, since I am a virgin?' And the angel answered her, 'The Holy Spirit will come upon you, and the power of the Most High will overshadow you; therefore the child to be born will be called holy—the Son of God. And behold, your relative Elizabeth in her old age has also conceived a son, and this is the sixth month with her who was called barren. For nothing will be impossible with God.' And Mary said, 'Behold, I am the servant of the Lord; let it be to me according to your word.' And the angel departed from her" (Luke 1:26-38, ESV).

Mary's acceptance of God's will is a direct contrast to Eve's disobedience. While Eve's action leads to the fall, Mary's obedience opens the way for salvation.

The Wedding at Cana: John 2:1-11

Mary's intercession at the wedding at Cana also highlights her role in the new creation:

"On the third day there was a wedding at Cana in Galilee, and the mother of Jesus was there. Jesus also was invited to the wedding with his disciples. When the wine ran out, the mother of Jesus said to him, 'They have no wine.' And Jesus said to her, 'Woman, what does this have to do with me? My hour has not yet come.' His mother said to the servants, 'Do whatever he tells you.' Now there were six stone water jars there for the Jewish rites of purification, each holding twenty or thirty gallons. Jesus said to the servants, 'Fill the jars with water.' And they filled them up to the brim. And he said to them, 'Now draw some out and take it to the master of the feast.' So they took it. When the master of the feast tasted the water now become wine, and did not know where it came from (though the servants who had drawn the water knew), the master of the feast called the bridegroom and said to him, 'Everyone serves the good wine first, and when people have drunk freely, then the poor wine. But you have kept the good wine until now.' This, the first of his signs, Jesus did at Cana in Galilee, and manifested his glory. And his disciples believed in him" (John 2:1-11, ESV).

Mary's role in this event illustrates her intercessory power and her participation in Jesus' mission. By addressing her as a "Woman," Jesus links her to the "woman" of Genesis 3:15, highlighting her role in the new creation.

The Crucifixion: John 19:25-27

Mary's presence at the crucifixion further underscores her role in the new creation:

"But standing by the cross of Jesus were his mother and his mother's sister, Mary the wife of Clopas, and Mary Magdalene. When Jesus saw his mother and the disciple whom he loved standing nearby, he said to his mother, 'Woman, behold, your son!' Then he said to the disciple, 'Behold, your mother!' And from that hour the disciple took her to his own home" (John 19:25-27, ESV).

By addressing her as "Woman" again, Jesus reinforces her connection to the prophecy in Genesis. Mary's participation in Jesus' suffering signifies her role in the new creation and the redemption of humanity.

Early Church Fathers on Mary as the New Eve

The early Church Fathers elaborated on the typology of Mary as the New Eve. St. Irenaeus of Lyons (c. 130-202 AD) is one of the earliest and most influential voices in this regard. In his work "Against Heresies," Irenaeus writes:

"The knot of Eve's disobedience was untied by Mary's obedience; what the virgin Eve bound through her disbelief, Mary loosened by her faith" (Against Heresies, Book 3, Chapter 22).

St. Justin Martyr (c. 100-165 AD) also draws a parallel between Eve and Mary:

"We know that He, before all creatures, proceeded from the Father by His power and will, and was born of a virgin as man, and that He endured all the afflictions that were foretold as destined to be inflicted on Him by the Jews, in order that, by this dispensation, the death inflicted by that serpent which was at first destroyed, and the power of the serpent brought to nought. For Eve, who was a virgin and undefiled, having conceived the word of the serpent, brought forth disobedience and death. But the Virgin Mary received faith and joy, when the angel Gabriel announced to her the glad tidings..." (Dialogue with Trypho, Chapter 100).

These writings illustrate the early Christian understanding of Mary's role as the New Eve, emphasizing her obedience and faith as crucial to the redemption narrative.

Biblical Evidence and Exhaustive Strong's Concordance Analysis

Using Strong's Exhaustive Concordance, we can examine the key terms and their implications:

- "Woman" (Greek: γυνή, gynē): This term is used by Jesus to address Mary in John 2:4 and John 19:26. It directly links her to the "woman" of Genesis 3:15, underscoring her role in the new creation.

- "Seed" (Greek: σπέρμα, sperma): In Genesis 3:15, the term "seed" refers to the offspring who will crush the serpent's head. Jesus, Mary's son, is this seed, fulfilling the prophecy and bringing redemption.

Comprehensive Commentary Insights

Comprehensive commentaries provide further insights into Mary's role as the New Eve:

- The New Jerome Biblical Commentary: This commentary emphasizes the parallel between Eve's disobedience and Mary's obedience, noting how Mary's acceptance of God's will contrasts with Eve's rejection.

- The Anchor Yale Bible Commentary: It highlights the theological significance of Mary's role in the Incarnation and her participation in Jesus' redemptive work, reinforcing the New Eve typology.

Conclusion: Mary as the New Eve

Mary's role as the New Eve is a central theme in Christian theology, highlighting her participation in God's redemptive plan. Her obedience and faith stand in stark contrast to Eve's disobedience, marking a new beginning through her son, Jesus Christ. The biblical evidence, supported by exhaustive concordances and comprehensive commentaries, underscores Mary's unique and pivotal role in salvation history.

Through Mary, the promise of Genesis 3:15 is fulfilled, bringing redemption and new life to humanity. Her participation in Jesus' mission, from the Annunciation to the Crucifixion, illustrates her integral role in the new creation, making her a model of faith and obedience for all believers.

CHAPTER 07

MARY AS THE NEW QUEEN MOTHER

The concept of the queen mother holds significant importance in ancient Near Eastern traditions, and this motif is richly woven into the fabric of biblical narratives. Mary, as the mother of Jesus, fits into this role within the kingdom of God in a profound way. This chapter will explore how Mary is the New Queen Mother, drawing on biblical evidence, exhaustive concordances, and comprehensive commentaries to understand her unique position in salvation history.

The Role of the Queen Mother in Ancient Israel

In the ancient Near East, particularly within the Davidic kingdom, the queen mother (Hebrew: גְּבִירָה, gebirah) held a special and influential position. Unlike many modern monarchies, where the queen consort holds a significant role, the queen mother in Israel had a recognized position of honor and authority.

One of the most prominent examples of the queen mother's role in Israel is Bathsheba, the mother of King Solomon. The narrative in 1 Kings 2:19 provides a clear example of her status:

"So Bathsheba went to King Solomon to speak to him on behalf of Adonijah. And the king rose to meet her and bowed down to her. Then he sat on his throne and had a seat brought for the king's mother, and she sat on his right" (1 Kings 2:19, ESV).

Solomon's treatment of Bathsheba exemplifies the respect and authority accorded to the queen mother. She had direct access to the king and could make intercessions on behalf of others, indicating her influential role in the royal court.

Mary as the New Queen Mother

In the New Testament, the role of the queen mother finds its ultimate fulfillment in Mary. As the mother of Jesus, the King of Kings, Mary assumes a position of unparalleled honor and significance.

The Annunciation: Luke 1:26-38

The angel Gabriel's announcement to Mary highlights her royal dignity and her son's kingship:

"And behold, you will conceive in your womb and bear a son, and you shall call his name Jesus. He will be great and will be called the Son of the Most High. And the Lord God will give to him the throne of his father David, and he will reign over the house of Jacob forever, and of his kingdom there will be no end" (Luke 1:31-33, ESV).

Mary's son is destined to inherit David's throne, establishing an everlasting kingdom. This prophecy underscores Mary's role as the queen mother in the new Davidic kingdom.

The Visit of the Magi: Matthew 2:11

The visit of the Magi further emphasizes Mary's royal status:

"And going into the house, they saw the child with Mary his mother, and they fell down and worshiped him. Then, opening their treasures, they offered him gifts, gold and frankincense and myrrh" (Matthew 2:11, ESV).

The Magi's reverence for the child and their recognition of his kingship inherently honor Mary, placing her in the position of the queen mother.

The Wedding at Cana: John 2:1-11

Mary's intercessory role at the wedding at Cana illustrates her influence and authority:

"When the wine ran out, the mother of Jesus said to him, 'They have no wine.' And Jesus said to her, 'Woman, what does this have to do with me? My hour has not yet come.' His mother said to the servants, 'Do whatever he tells you'" (John 2:3-5, ESV).

Mary's ability to intercede and her confidence in Jesus' response highlight her unique position. Jesus' address of Mary as "Woman" links her to the "woman" of Genesis 3:15 and emphasizes her role in the new creation.

The Crucifixion: John 19:25-27

Mary's presence at the crucifixion and Jesus' words to her and the beloved disciple further illustrate her role:

"When Jesus saw his mother and the disciple whom he loved standing nearby, he said to his mother, 'Woman, behold, your son!' Then he said to the disciple, 'Behold, your mother!' And from that hour the disciple took her to his own home" (John 19:26-27, ESV).

Jesus' designation of Mary as the mother of the beloved disciple extends her maternal role to all believers, reinforcing her status as the spiritual queen mother of the Church.

Strong's Exhaustive Concordance Analysis

Using Strong's Exhaustive Concordance, we can delve deeper into the terms that illustrate Mary's role as the queen mother:

- "Woman" (Greek: γυνή, gynē): This term is used by Jesus to address Mary in John 2:4 and John 19:26, linking her to the "woman" of Genesis 3:15 and highlighting her role in the new creation.

- "Mother" (Greek: μήτηρ, mētēr): This term, used frequently in reference to Mary, emphasizes her maternal authority and care, both in a biological and spiritual sense.

Comprehensive Commentary Insights

Comprehensive commentaries provide further insights into Mary's role as the queen mother:

- The New Jerome Biblical Commentary: This commentary highlights the significance of Mary's intercessory role and her position within the royal Davidic line, drawing parallels to the queen mothers of the Old Testament.

- The Anchor Yale Bible Commentary: It emphasizes Mary's unique status as the mother of Jesus, the Messiah, and her participation in His redemptive mission, reinforcing her role as the queen mother.

Theological Implications

The theological implications of Mary as the queen mother are profound:

1. Intercessory Role: Mary's position as queen mother grants her a special role in interceding for the faithful. Just as Bathsheba interceded on behalf of others in the royal court, Mary intercedes for believers, as seen at the wedding at Cana and affirmed in various Church traditions.

2. Maternal Care: Mary's designation as the mother of all believers emphasizes her ongoing spiritual motherhood. This is reflected in her care and concern for the Church, mirroring the protective and nurturing role of a queen mother.

3. Participation in the Kingdom: Mary's role in the kingdom of God underscores her active participation in the establishment and continuation of Jesus' reign. Her unique position highlights the dignity and honor accorded to her within the divine plan.

Conclusion: Mary as the New Queen Mother

Mary's role as the New Queen Mother is a central theme in Christian theology, drawing on the ancient Near Eastern tradition of the queen mother. Her unique position as the mother of Jesus, the King of Kings, grants her unparalleled honor and influence within the kingdom of God.

Through biblical evidence, exhaustive concordance analysis, and comprehensive commentary insights, we gain a deeper understanding of Mary's role. Her intercessory power, maternal care, and participation in Jesus' mission exemplify her status as the queen mother, making her a model of faith and devotion for all believers.

By recognizing Mary as the New Queen Mother, we can appreciate her significant role in salvation history and her ongoing influence in the life of the Church. Her unique position highlights the continuity of God's redemptive work and the fulfillment of ancient promises through her son, Jesus Christ.

CHAPTER 08

MARY AS THE NEW ARK OF THE COVENANT

The Ark of the Covenant is one of the most significant and sacred objects in the Old Testament, representing the presence of God among His people. In Christian theology, Mary is often compared to the Ark of the Covenant, as she bore the presence of God within her womb. This chapter will explore this typology, examining the theological significance of Mary as the New Ark of the Covenant, supported by biblical evidence, exhaustive concordance analysis, and comprehensive commentary.

The Ark of the Covenant in the Old Testament

The Ark of the Covenant was a sacred chest built by the Israelites under the direction of Moses, as described in Exodus 25. It contained the tablets of the Law, Aaron's rod that budded, and a golden urn holding manna (Hebrews 9:4). The Ark symbolized God's covenant with Israel and His presence among them.

The specifications and instructions for the Ark highlight its sacred nature:

"They shall make an ark of acacia wood. Two cubits and a half shall be its length, a cubit and a half its breadth, and a cubit and a half its height. You shall overlay it with pure gold, inside and outside shall you overlay it, and you shall make on it a molding of gold around it" (Exodus 25:10-11, ESV).

The Ark was placed in the Holy of Holies, the innermost and most sacred area of the Tabernacle, where God's presence dwelled. Only the high priest could enter this space once a year on the Day of Atonement to make atonement for the sins of the people.

Mary as the New Ark of the Covenant

The New Testament presents Mary as the fulfillment of the Ark's typology. Several key passages highlight this parallel, demonstrating how Mary, as the bearer of God's presence, fulfills the role of the Ark.

The Annunciation: Luke 1:26-38

The angel Gabriel's announcement to Mary that she would conceive and bear the Son of God parallels the indwelling presence of God in the Ark:

"And the angel said to her, 'Do not be afraid, Mary, for you have found favor with God. And behold, you will conceive in your womb and bear a son, and you shall call his name Jesus. He will be great and will be called the Son of the Most High. And the Lord God will give to him the throne of his father David, and he will reign over the house of Jacob forever, and of his kingdom there will be no end.' And Mary said to the angel, 'How will this be, since I am a virgin?' And the angel answered her, 'The Holy Spirit will come upon you, and the power of the Most High will overshadow you; therefore the child to be born will be called holy—the Son of God'" (Luke 1:30-35, ESV).

The term "overshadow" (Greek: ἐπισκιάσει, episkiasei) is the same word used in the Septuagint (the Greek translation of the Old Testament) to describe God's presence overshadowing the Ark (Exodus 40:34-35). This indicates that just as the Ark was the dwelling place of God's presence, so Mary would be the new dwelling place for God incarnate.

The Visitation: Luke 1:39-45

The account of Mary's visit to Elizabeth further underscores the parallel between Mary and the Ark:

"In those days Mary arose and went with haste into the hill country, to a town in Judah, and she entered the house of Zechariah and greeted Elizabeth. And when Elizabeth heard the greeting of Mary, the baby leaped in her womb. And Elizabeth was filled with the Holy Spirit, and she exclaimed with a loud cry, 'Blessed are you among women, and blessed is the fruit of your womb! And why is this granted to me that the mother of my Lord should come to me? For behold, when the sound of your greeting came to my ears, the baby in my womb leaped for joy. And blessed is she who believed that there would be a fulfillment of what was spoken to her from the Lord'" (Luke 1:39-45, ESV).

Elizabeth's reaction mirrors the response of David when the Ark was brought to Jerusalem:

"And David was afraid of the Lord that day, and he said, 'How can the ark of the Lord come to me?'" (2 Samuel 6:9, ESV).

Both Mary's and the Ark's journeys into the hill country, their reception, and the joy they bring emphasize Mary's role as the New Ark.

Revelation 11:19-12:1

The Book of Revelation also makes a striking connection between Mary and the Ark:

"Then God's temple in heaven was opened, and the ark of his covenant was seen within his temple. There were flashes of lightning, rumblings, peals of thunder, an earthquake, and heavy hail. And a great sign appeared in heaven: a woman clothed with the sun, with the moon under her feet, and on her head a crown of twelve stars" (Revelation 11:19-12:1, ESV).

The vision of the Ark of the Covenant immediately followed by the vision of the woman clothed with the sun suggests a symbolic link between Mary and the Ark. The woman represents Mary, the mother of the Messiah, reinforcing her role as the New Ark.

Strong's Exhaustive Concordance Analysis

Using Strong's Exhaustive Concordance, we can further explore the key terms and their theological implications:

- "Overshadow" (Greek: ἐπισκιάζω, episkiazō): This term is used to describe the Holy Spirit's action in both Luke 1:35 and Exodus 40:35, linking the presence of God in the Ark with His presence in Mary.

- "Ark" (Hebrew: אֲרוֹן, ʾārôn): The term denotes the sacred chest containing the covenant items, signifying God's dwelling place. In the New Testament, Mary becomes the living Ark, bearing Jesus, the Word made flesh.

Comprehensive Commentary Insights

Comprehensive commentaries provide deeper insights into Mary as the New Ark:

- The New Jerome Biblical Commentary: This commentary highlights the parallels between Mary and the Ark, emphasizing the theological significance of Mary's role as the bearer of God's presence.

- The Anchor Yale Bible Commentary: It explores the typology of Mary as the New Ark, noting how her actions and experiences mirror those associated with the Ark of the Covenant.

Theological Implications

The theological implications of Mary as the New Ark of the Covenant are profound:

1. God's Presence: Just as the Ark was the dwelling place of God's presence among the Israelites, Mary, by bearing Jesus, becomes the new dwelling place of God's presence on earth. This underscores the Incarnation's significance and the intimate connection between God and humanity.

2. Holiness and Purity: The Ark was made of acacia wood and overlaid with pure gold, symbolizing its holiness.

Mary's purity and her being "full of grace" (Luke 1:28) reflect the sanctity required to bear God's presence.

3. Intercession and Mediation: The Ark was a point of mediation between God and His people, especially during the Day of Atonement. Mary's role as the New Ark underscores her intercessory power, as seen at the wedding at Cana and throughout Christian tradition.

Conclusion: Mary as the New Ark of the Covenant

Mary's role as the New Ark of the Covenant is a central theme in Christian theology, reflecting her unique position as the bearer of God's presence. The biblical evidence, supported by exhaustive concordance analysis and comprehensive commentary insights, highlights the deep typological connection between Mary and the Ark.

Through Mary, the promises and presence of God are brought into the world in a tangible and transformative way. Her role as the New Ark emphasizes the Incarnation's profound mystery and the intimate relationship between God and humanity.

By recognizing Mary as the New Ark of the Covenant, we gain a deeper appreciation for her significance in salvation history and her ongoing influence in the life of the Church. Her unique position highlights the continuity of God's redemptive work and the fulfillment of ancient promises through her son, Jesus Christ.

58

CHAPTER 09

MARY AS THE WOMAN CLOTHED WITH THE SUN

The imagery of the woman clothed with the sun in Revelation 12 is one of the most striking and symbolically rich passages in the New Testament. This chapter will explore how this image applies to Mary, delving into its symbolism and roots in Jewish apocalyptic literature, supported by biblical evidence, exhaustive concordance analysis, and comprehensive commentary.

The Vision in Revelation 12

The key passage that describes the woman clothed with the sun is found in Revelation 12:1-6:

"And a great sign appeared in heaven: a woman clothed with the sun, with the moon under her feet, and on her head a crown of twelve stars. She was pregnant and was crying out in birth pains and the agony of giving birth. And another sign appeared in heaven: behold, a great red dragon, with seven heads and ten horns, and on his heads seven diadems. His tail swept down a third of the stars of heaven and cast them to the earth. And the dragon stood before the woman who was about to give birth, so that when she bore her child he might devour it. She gave birth to a male child, one who is to rule all the nations with a rod of iron, but her child was caught up to God and to his throne, and the woman fled into the wilderness, where she has a place prepared by God, in which she is to be nourished for 1,260 days" (Revelation 12:1-6, ESV).

This passage is rich with symbolic elements that have been interpreted in various ways throughout Christian history. While the woman can be seen as representing Israel, the Church, and Mary, this chapter will focus on the Marian interpretation.

Symbolism of the Woman Clothed with the Sun

Clothed with the Sun

The description of the woman being clothed with the sun signifies her glory, radiance, and exalted status. In the context of Mary, this imagery highlights her unique role and honor as the mother of the Messiah.

The Moon Under Her Feet

The moon under her feet symbolizes her dominion and victory over change and instability, as the moon is associated with these concepts in ancient symbolism. For Mary, this indicates her triumph over sin and death, particularly through her Assumption into heaven.

Crown of Twelve Stars

The crown of twelve stars represents the twelve tribes of Israel, connecting Mary to the people of God. It also signifies her queenship, as she is often referred to as the Queen of Heaven in Catholic tradition.

Birth Pains and the Dragon

The woman's birth pains and the presence of the dragon reflect the trials and opposition faced by Mary and the Church. The dragon's attempt to devour the child signifies Satan's opposition to Jesus and His mission. Mary's protection of her child and her role in God's plan highlight her courage and faithfulness.

Jewish Apocalyptic Literature

The imagery in Revelation 12 draws on themes and symbols common in Jewish apocalyptic literature, which often used vivid and dramatic imagery to convey spiritual truths and prophetic visions.

Woman and Child

The motif of a woman giving birth to a significant child appears in various Jewish texts. For example, Isaiah 66:7-8 speaks of Zion giving birth to her children, symbolizing the nation of Israel bringing forth the Messiah:

"Before she was in labor she gave birth; before her pain came upon her she delivered a son. Who has heard such a thing? Who has seen such things? Shall a land be born in one day? Shall a nation be brought forth in one moment? For as soon as Zion was in labor she brought forth her children" (Isaiah 66:7-8, ESV).

The Dragon

The dragon in Revelation 12 is reminiscent of the chaos monsters in ancient Near Eastern mythology, such as Leviathan in the Hebrew Bible:

"In that day the Lord with his hard and great and strong sword will punish Leviathan the fleeing serpent, Leviathan the twisting serpent, and he will slay the dragon that is in the sea" (Isaiah 27:1, ESV).

This imagery symbolizes the forces of chaos and evil opposing God's plan, further connecting the woman to the cosmic struggle between good and evil.

Strong's Exhaustive Concordance Analysis

Using Strong's Exhaustive Concordance, we can analyze key terms in Revelation 12 to deepen our understanding:

- "Woman" (Greek: γυνή, gynē): The term is used to denote both the general concept of a woman and, in this context, a specific figure with a significant role in salvation history. The consistent use of "woman" in connection with Mary (e.g., John 2:4; John 19:26) supports her identification with the woman in Revelation 12.

- "Dragon" (Greek: δράκων, drakōn): The dragon symbolizes Satan (Revelation 12:9), representing the spiritual adversary against whom Mary's child, Jesus, triumphs.

Comprehensive Commentary Insights

Comprehensive commentaries provide further insights into Mary as the woman clothed with the sun:

- The New Jerome Biblical Commentary: This commentary discusses the multi-layered symbolism of the woman, acknowledging the Marian interpretation and emphasizing her role in the cosmic battle between good and evil.

- The Anchor Yale Bible Commentary: It explores the apocalyptic imagery in Revelation, noting the parallels between the woman and key figures in Jewish apocalyptic literature, while highlighting Mary's significance in this context.

Theological Implications

The theological implications of Mary as the woman clothed with the sun are significant:

1. Marian Devotion: Recognizing Mary in this role enhances her veneration as a key figure in salvation history, reflecting her exalted status and intercessory power.

2. Spiritual Warfare: The imagery underscores Mary's role in the spiritual battle against evil, highlighting her participation in the victory of Christ over Satan.

3. Queenship: The crown of twelve stars and the sun's radiance affirm Mary's queenship, emphasizing her unique position in the divine plan and her relationship with the people of God.

Conclusion: Mary as the Woman Clothed with the Sun

Mary's identification with the woman clothed with the sun in Revelation 12 is a powerful and theologically rich interpretation. The biblical evidence, supported by exhaustive concordance analysis and comprehensive commentary insights, highlights the depth of this typology.

Mary's role as the woman clothed with the sun underscores her participation in God's redemptive plan, her victory over evil, and her exalted status as the Queen of Heaven. This imagery not only enriches our understanding of Mary but also deepens our appreciation for her ongoing influence and intercession in the life of the Church.

By recognizing Mary as the woman clothed with the sun, we can better appreciate her significance in salvation history and her unique contribution to the fulfillment of God's promises through her son, Jesus Christ. Her role in the cosmic struggle against evil and her maternal care for all believers reflect her enduring legacy and profound importance in Christian theology.

CHAPTER 10

MARY IN THE EARLY CHRISTIN WRITINGS

The early Christian writings provide invaluable insights into how the first generations of Christians viewed Mary, the mother of Jesus. This chapter will survey the writings of the Church Fathers and other early Christian texts to understand the development of Marian doctrine and devotion. We will also examine the biblical foundations for these views, supported by exhaustive concordance analysis and comprehensive commentary.

The Protoevangelium of James

One of the earliest and most influential apocryphal texts that provide details about Mary's life is the Protoevangelium of James, written around the mid-2nd century. This text offers an expanded narrative of Mary's birth, upbringing, and betrothal to Joseph. While not part of the canonical scriptures, it significantly shaped early Christian thought about Mary.

Key points from the Protoevangelium of James include:

- Mary's Immaculate Conception: The text emphasizes Mary's purity from birth, an idea that would later develop into the doctrine of the Immaculate Conception.

- Mary's Perpetual Virginity: It highlights her vow of virginity and her miraculous conception of Jesus, supporting the belief in Mary's perpetual virginity.

Ignatius of Antioch (c. 35-108 AD)

Ignatius, an early Church Father and bishop of Antioch, wrote several letters that mention Mary. In his letter to the Ephesians, Ignatius underscores the reality of Jesus' human birth and Mary's role in the Incarnation:

"For our God, Jesus Christ, was conceived by Mary in accord with God's plan: of the seed of David, it is true, but also of the Holy Spirit" (Ignatius of Antioch, Letter to the Ephesians, 18:2).

Ignatius' writings affirm the belief in the virgin birth and Mary's essential role in the divine plan of salvation.

Justin Martyr (c. 100-165 AD)

Justin Martyr, an early Christian apologist, drew a parallel between Eve and Mary, describing Mary as the New Eve. In his "Dialogue with Trypho," Justin writes:

"For Eve, who was a virgin and undefiled, having conceived the word of the serpent, brought forth disobedience and death. But the Virgin Mary received faith and joy, when the angel Gabriel announced to her the glad tidings..." (Dialogue with Trypho, 100).

This typology highlights Mary's obedience and faith, contrasting it with Eve's disobedience, and establishing Mary's role in the redemption narrative.

Irenaeus of Lyons (c. 130-202 AD)

Irenaeus, a key theological figure, also emphasized Mary's role as the New Eve in his work "Against Heresies":

"The knot of Eve's disobedience was untied by Mary's obedience; what the virgin Eve bound through her disbelief, Mary loosened by her faith" (Against Heresies, 3:22:4).

Irenaeus' writings further solidify the parallel between Eve and Mary, highlighting Mary's pivotal role in God's redemptive plan.

Tertullian (c. 160-225 AD)

Tertullian, an early Christian writer, defended the doctrine of the virgin birth and emphasized Mary's role in the Incarnation. In "On the Flesh of Christ," he writes:

"God sent down into the virgin's womb His Spirit, though even then He did not dismiss His Word, but made it assume the flesh of our nature, which, by means of the womb of the virgin, He forthwith wove into Himself" (On the Flesh of Christ, 18).

Tertullian's work underscores the miraculous nature of Jesus' conception and Mary's essential participation in the Incarnation.

Origen (c. 184-253 AD)

Origen, one of the most prolific early Christian scholars, wrote extensively about Mary. In his homilies on Luke, Origen reflects on Mary's role and her virtues:

"Mary is worthy of being admired and emulated for the way she listened to the word of God and kept it in her heart. She conceived the Word in her mind before she conceived Him in her womb" (Homilies on Luke, 6).

Origen's reflections emphasize Mary's spiritual receptivity and her role as a model disciple who faithfully followed God's will.

Athanasius of Alexandria (c. 296-373 AD)

Athanasius, a staunch defender of Nicene orthodoxy, also wrote about Mary's significance. In his work "On the Incarnation," he highlights the mystery of the Word becoming flesh through Mary:

"He took to Himself a body, a body truly animated by a rational soul, that He, being thus incarnate, might offer it as His own in the stead of all men" (On the Incarnation, 8).

Athanasius' writings affirm the centrality of the Incarnation and Mary's crucial role in this divine mystery.

Strong's Exhaustive Concordance Analysis

Using Strong's Exhaustive Concordance, we can examine key biblical terms related to Mary:

- "Virgin" (Greek: παρθένος, parthenos): This term is used in the Annunciation narrative (Luke 1:27) to describe Mary, emphasizing her purity and the miraculous nature of Jesus' conception.

- "Mother" (Greek: μήτηρ, mētēr): This term is used frequently in the Gospels to denote Mary's maternal role, highlighting her relationship with Jesus (e.g., Matthew 1:18; John 19:25-27).

Comprehensive Commentary Insights

Comprehensive commentaries provide deeper insights into the early Christian understanding of Mary:

- The New Jerome Biblical Commentary: This commentary discusses the development of Marian doctrine and the early Church Fathers' contributions to Marian theology.

- The Anchor Yale Bible Commentary: It explores the biblical foundations for Marian beliefs and how early Christian texts reflect and expand upon these foundations.

Theological Development and Implications

The early Christian writings reveal a progressive development in Marian doctrine and devotion:

1. Virgin Birth: The belief in Mary's virginal conception of Jesus is consistently affirmed, highlighting the miraculous nature of the Incarnation.

2. Mary as the New Eve: The typological parallel between Eve and Mary is a recurring theme, emphasizing Mary's role in reversing the disobedience of Eve through her obedience and faith.

3. Perpetual Virginity: Early texts, like the Protoevangelium of James, lay the groundwork for the doctrine of Mary's perpetual virginity.

4. Spiritual Motherhood: The early Church recognized Mary's spiritual motherhood, extending her maternal care to all believers, as seen in John 19:26-27.

Conclusion: Mary in the Early Christian Writings

The early Christian writings provide a rich and nuanced understanding of Mary's role in salvation history. Through the writings of the Church Fathers and other early texts, we see the development of key Marian doctrines, such as her virgin birth, her role as the New Eve, and her perpetual virginity.

These writings highlight the profound respect and veneration early Christians had for Mary, recognizing her unique role in God's redemptive plan. By examining the biblical evidence, supported by exhaustive concordance analysis and comprehensive commentary insights, we gain a deeper appreciation for Mary's significance in the early Church and her ongoing influence in Christian theology.

Through the lens of these early writings, we can better understand the foundations of Marian devotion and the theological depth of her role as the mother of Jesus and a model of faith for all believers.

CHAPTER 11

THE EVOLUTION OF MARIAN THEOLOGY IN THE CHURCH

The development of Marian theology has been a dynamic process, evolving from the early Church through the Middle Ages and into the modern era. This chapter will trace this evolution, examining key doctrinal developments, theological debates, and the impact of Marian devotion on Christian thought and practice. We will explore biblical evidence, supported by exhaustive concordance analysis and comprehensive commentary, to understand the progression of Marian theology.

Early Church (1st to 5th Centuries)

The early Church laid the foundational principles of Marian theology, drawing on Scripture and the writings of the Church Fathers.

The Council of Ephesus (431 AD)

One of the most significant early developments was the Council of Ephesus, which affirmed Mary's title as Theotokos (Greek: Θεοτόκος), meaning "God-bearer" or "Mother of God." This declaration was crucial in affirming the divine and human natures of Jesus Christ:

"We confess, then, our Lord Jesus Christ, the only-begotten Son of God, perfect God and perfect man... born for us and for our salvation of Mary the Virgin, Theotokos" (Council of Ephesus, 431 AD).

This title emphasized Mary's role in the Incarnation and safeguarded the doctrine of Jesus' divinity.

Patristic Writings

The writings of the Church Fathers, such as Ignatius of Antioch, Justin Martyr, Irenaeus, Tertullian, and Origen, contributed significantly to early Marian theology, as discussed in Chapter 10. Their reflections on Mary's role as the New Eve and her perpetual virginity laid important theological groundwork.

Middle Ages (6th to 15th Centuries)

The Middle Ages saw a flourishing of Marian devotion and the formalization of key doctrines.

The Immaculate Conception

The doctrine of the Immaculate Conception, which teaches that Mary was conceived without original sin, began to take shape during this period. St. Anselm of Canterbury (1033-1109) and other theologians argued for Mary's unique sanctity:

"It was fitting that the Virgin should be adorned with the greatest purity" (Anselm, De Conceptu Virginali).

The feast of the Immaculate Conception was celebrated in various parts of Europe, reflecting growing devotion to this belief.

The Assumption

The belief in Mary's Assumption, the teaching that Mary was taken body and soul into heaven at the end of her earthly life, also gained prominence. St. John of Damascus (676-749) was a key proponent:

"It was fitting that she, who had kept her virginity in childbirth, should keep her own body free from all corruption even after death" (John of Damascus, Homily on the Dormition).

This belief was celebrated in the liturgy and popular piety long before its formal definition.

Marian Devotion

The Middle Ages witnessed a proliferation of Marian devotion, including the development of the rosary, Marian hymns, and feast days. St. Bernard of Clairvaux (1090-1153) was a notable figure in promoting Marian devotion:

"Let us not imagine that we obscure the glory of the Son by the great praise we lavish on the Mother; for the more she is honored, the greater is the glory of her Son" (St. Bernard, Homily on the Missus Est).

Renaissance and Reformation (16th to 17th Centuries)

The Renaissance period continued the tradition of Marian devotion, but the Reformation brought significant challenges and changes.

Protestant Reformation

The Protestant Reformation led by Martin Luther, John Calvin, and other reformers questioned many traditional practices, including certain aspects of Marian devotion. While Luther retained a high view of Mary's role in salvation history, he rejected the invocation of saints and the doctrine of the Immaculate Conception:

"Mary is the highest woman and the noblest gem in Christianity after Christ... She is nobility, wisdom, and holiness personified" (Martin Luther, Sermon on the Feast of the Visitation).

However, Marian devotion was largely diminished in Protestant traditions, focusing instead on scriptural foundations and personal faith.

Catholic Counter-Reformation

The Catholic Counter-Reformation reaffirmed Marian doctrines and devotion. The Council of Trent (1545-1563) emphasized the importance of Marian intercession and upheld traditional beliefs:

"The saints who reign together with Christ offer up their own prayers to God for men. It is good and useful suppliantly to invoke them" (Council of Trent, Session 25).

This period saw the continuation and expansion of Marian art, literature, and theological works.

Modern Era (18th Century to Present)

The modern era has seen further development and formalization of Marian doctrines, along with an increase in Marian apparitions and devotions.

The Immaculate Conception (1854)

Pope Pius IX formally defined the doctrine of the Immaculate Conception in the apostolic constitution "Ineffabilis Deus":

"We declare, pronounce, and define that the doctrine which holds that the most Blessed Virgin Mary, in the first instance of her conception... was preserved free from all stain of original sin" (Ineffabilis Deus, 1854).

This declaration affirmed the long-held belief in Mary's unique sanctity and purity.

The Assumption (1950)

Pope Pius XII defined the doctrine of the Assumption in the apostolic constitution "Munificentissimus Deus":

"We pronounce, declare, and define it to be a divinely revealed dogma: that the Immaculate Mother of God, the ever Virgin Mary, having completed the course of her earthly life, was assumed body and soul into heavenly glory" (Munificentissimus Deus, 1950).

This dogma formalized the belief in Mary's Assumption, celebrated for centuries in the Church's liturgy.

Marian Apparitions

The modern era has also seen numerous Marian apparitions, including those at Lourdes (1858) and Fatima (1917), which have significantly influenced Marian devotion and theology. These apparitions often emphasize Mary's role as intercessor and her call to prayer and repentance.

Strong's Exhaustive Concordance Analysis

Using Strong's Exhaustive Concordance, we can explore key terms related to Marian theology:

- "Grace" (Greek: χάρις, charis): This term is used in Luke 1:28 ("full of grace") to describe Mary, emphasizing her unique favor with God.

- "Blessed" (Greek: εὐλογημένη, eulogēmenē): This term, used in Luke 1:42, highlights Mary's blessedness among women, reflecting her honored status.

Comprehensive Commentary Insights

Comprehensive commentaries provide deeper insights into the development of Marian theology:

- The New Jerome Biblical Commentary: This commentary explores the historical and theological evolution of Marian doctrines, highlighting key developments and controversies.

- The Anchor Yale Bible Commentary: It offers detailed analysis of biblical texts related to Mary and how these texts have been interpreted throughout Church history.

Conclusion: The Evolution of Marian Theology

The evolution of Marian theology from the early Church through the Middle Ages and into the modern era reflects a dynamic and ongoing process of doctrinal development and deepening devotion. Key milestones, such as the Council of Ephesus, the definitions of the Immaculate

Conception and the Assumption, and the influence of Marian apparitions, have shaped the Church's understanding and veneration of Mary.

By tracing this evolution, we gain a deeper appreciation for the richness and complexity of Marian theology. The biblical foundations, supported by exhaustive concordance analysis and comprehensive commentary insights, underscore the continuity and development of Marian beliefs across centuries.

Through this exploration, we see how Mary's role as the Mother of God, the New Eve, and the Queen of Heaven has been understood and celebrated in diverse ways, reflecting her central place in the Christian faith and her ongoing significance in the life of the Church.

CHAPTER 12

MARY IN CATHOLIC THEOLOGY

Catholic theology holds Mary, the mother of Jesus, in a place of high honor and reverence. Several key doctrines and teachings articulate her unique role in salvation history and the life of the Church. This chapter will provide an overview of Catholic teachings on Mary, including the doctrines of the Immaculate Conception, the Assumption, and her role as intercessor. We will explore the biblical foundations of these beliefs, supported by exhaustive concordance analysis and comprehensive commentary.

The Immaculate Conception

The doctrine of the Immaculate Conception teaches that Mary was conceived without original sin. This belief was formally defined by Pope Pius IX in 1854 in the apostolic constitution "Ineffabilis Deus":

"We declare, pronounce, and define that the doctrine which holds that the most Blessed Virgin Mary, in the first instance of her conception... was preserved free from all stain of original sin" (Ineffabilis Deus, 1854).

Biblical Foundations

The biblical foundation for the Immaculate Conception is often traced to the angel Gabriel's greeting to Mary at the Annunciation:

"And he came to her and said, 'Greetings, O favored one, the Lord is with you!'" (Luke 1:28, ESV).

The term "favored one" (Greek: κεχαριτωμένη, kecharitōmenē) can be translated as "full of grace." This phrase suggests a unique grace given to Mary, interpreted by Catholic theology as her preservation from original sin from the moment of her conception.

Strong's Exhaustive Concordance Analysis

-     "Favored   one"   (Greek: κεχαριτωμένη, kecharitōmenē): This term indicates being endowed with grace, suggesting a special divine favor.

Comprehensive Commentary Insights

- The New Jerome Biblical Commentary: This commentary notes that the phrase "full of grace" indicates Mary's unique role and the special grace she received from God.

- The Anchor Yale Bible Commentary: It highlights the theological implications of the angel's greeting and the longstanding tradition of interpreting this phrase as a reference to Mary's immaculate state.

The Assumption

The doctrine of the Assumption teaches that Mary was taken body and soul into heavenly glory at the end of her earthly life. This belief was formally defined by Pope Pius XII in 1950 in the apostolic constitution "Munificentissimus Deus":

"We pronounce, declare, and define it to be a divinely revealed dogma: that the Immaculate Mother of God, the ever Virgin Mary, having completed the course of her earthly life, was assumed body and soul into heavenly glory" (Munificentissimus Deus, 1950).

Biblical Foundations

While there is no direct biblical account of the Assumption, Catholic theology sees implicit support in several passages. One such passage is found in Revelation:

"Then God's temple in heaven was opened, and the ark of his covenant was seen within his temple. There were flashes of lightning, rumblings, peals of thunder, an earthquake, and heavy hail. And a great sign appeared in heaven: a woman clothed with the sun, with the moon under her feet, and on her head a crown of twelve stars" (Revelation 11:19-12:1, ESV).

The woman clothed with the sun is often interpreted as Mary, symbolizing her exaltation and glorification.

Strong's Exhaustive Concordance Analysis

- "Woman" (Greek: γυνή, gynē): Used in Revelation 12:1, this term links to Mary and her exalted status in heaven.

- "Ark of his covenant" (Greek: κιβωτός τῆς διαθήκης, kibōtos tēs diathēkēs): Symbolically linked to Mary as the New Ark, bearing Jesus.

Comprehensive Commentary Insights

- The New Jerome Biblical Commentary: This commentary discusses the symbolic interpretation of the woman in Revelation as Mary, supporting the theological basis for the Assumption.

- The Anchor Yale Bible Commentary: It explores the connections between Marian symbolism in Revelation and the tradition of the Assumption.

Mary as Intercessor

Catholic theology holds that Mary, as the Mother of God and Queen of Heaven, intercedes for believers. This belief is rooted in her unique relationship with Jesus and her role in the communion of saints.

Biblical Foundations

The biblical foundation for Mary's intercessory role includes her actions at the Wedding at Cana:

"When the wine ran out, the mother of Jesus said to him, 'They have no wine.' And Jesus said to her, 'Woman, what does this have to do with me? My hour has not yet come.' His mother said to the servants, 'Do whatever he tells you'" (John 2:3-5, ESV).

Mary's intercession leads to Jesus performing His first miracle, highlighting her role in mediating between the people and her son.

Strong's Exhaustive Concordance Analysis

- "Woman" (Greek: γυνή, gynē): Jesus' address of Mary as "woman" links her to the intercessory role suggested in Genesis 3:15 and Revelation 12.

- "Do whatever he tells you" (Greek: ποιήσατε ὅτι ἂν λέγῃ ὑμῖν, poiēsate hoti an legē hymin): Mary's directive indicates her confidence in Jesus' divine mission and her role in prompting His actions.

Comprehensive Commentary Insights

- The New Jerome Biblical Commentary: This commentary highlights Mary's role at Cana as indicative of her intercessory power and her influence in Jesus' ministry.

- The Anchor Yale Bible Commentary: It discusses the significance of Mary's intercession and its theological implications for her ongoing role in the Church.

Marian Titles and Devotions

Catholic theology ascribes various titles to Mary that reflect her unique role and attributes, including:

- Theotokos (Mother of God): Affirmed at the Council of Ephesus, emphasizing her role in the Incarnation.

- Queen of Heaven: Reflecting her exalted status and intercessory role.

- Our Lady of Perpetual Help, Our Lady of Guadalupe, and other Marian titles: Reflecting her ongoing presence and aid in the lives of believers.

Devotions such as the Rosary, Marian feasts, and Marian prayers (e.g., the Hail Mary) are integral to Catholic practice, emphasizing Mary's role as a model of faith and a powerful intercessor.

Conclusion: Mary in Catholic Theology

Mary's role in Catholic theology is rich and multifaceted, encompassing doctrines such as the Immaculate Conception, the Assumption, and her intercessory power.

These beliefs are rooted in biblical foundations, supported by exhaustive concordance analysis and comprehensive commentary insights.

Through these teachings, the Catholic Church honors Mary's unique role in salvation history and her ongoing influence in the life of the Church. Her example of faith, obedience, and maternal care continues to inspire and guide believers, reflecting her central place in Catholic devotion and theology.

By understanding these doctrines and their biblical and theological bases, we gain a deeper appreciation for Mary's significance and the profound reverence accorded to her within the Catholic tradition. Her role as the Mother of God, the New Eve, and the Queen of Heaven underscores her pivotal place in God's redemptive plan and her enduring legacy in the Christian faith.

CHAPTER 13

MARY IN PROTESTANT THEOLOGY

The Protestant Reformation brought about significant changes in the theological landscape, including perspectives on Mary, the mother of Jesus. This chapter will examine the Protestant view of Mary, highlighting key theological differences and areas of agreement with Catholic doctrine. We will explore the biblical foundations for these views, supported by exhaustive concordance analysis and comprehensive commentary.

The Reformation Context

The Protestant Reformation, initiated by figures like Martin Luther, John Calvin, and Huldrych Zwingli, aimed to address various doctrinal and ecclesiastical issues within the Catholic Church. This movement led to a reevaluation of many traditional practices and beliefs, including the veneration of Mary.

Martin Luther (1483-1546)

Martin Luther retained a high regard for Mary, emphasizing her role as the Mother of God (Theotokos) while rejecting certain Catholic doctrines and practices. He upheld the virgin birth and Mary's perpetual virginity but critiqued the invocation of saints and the belief in Mary's immaculate conception:

"Mary is the highest woman and the noblest gem in Christianity after Christ... She is nobility, wisdom, and holiness personified. We can never honor her enough" (Martin Luther, Sermon on the Feast of the Visitation).

John Calvin (1509-1564)

John Calvin respected Mary's role in the Incarnation but was critical of what he saw as excessive veneration. He emphasized the importance of focusing on Christ rather than on saints:

"We cannot proclaim the praises of Mary without obscuring the glory of Christ" (John Calvin, Commentary on Luke).

Calvin acknowledged Mary's blessedness and unique role but insisted that she should not be an object of prayer or intercession.

Huldrych Zwingli (1484-1531)

Huldrych Zwingli also affirmed the doctrine of Mary's perpetual virginity, aligning with some traditional views while rejecting others:

"I firmly believe that Mary, according to the words of the Gospel, as a pure Virgin brought forth for us the Son of God and in childbirth and after childbirth forever remained a pure, intact Virgin" (Zwingli, Letter to a Friend).

Key Theological Differences

The Immaculate Conception

Protestants generally reject the doctrine of the Immaculate Conception, viewing it as lacking clear biblical support. Instead, they emphasize the universality of sin, including Mary's need for salvation:

"For all have sinned and fall short of the glory of God" (Romans 3:23, ESV).

Protestant theology maintains that only Christ was sinless, and Mary, like all humans, needed redemption through Him.

The Assumption

The doctrine of the Assumption is also not accepted in Protestant theology, as it is not explicitly supported by Scripture. Protestants focus on the biblical text and are cautious about doctrines developed from tradition rather than clear biblical evidence.

Intercession and Marian Devotion

Protestants reject the practice of praying to Mary and the saints, emphasizing the sole mediatorship of Christ:

"For there is one God, and there is one mediator between God and men, the man Christ Jesus" (1 Timothy 2:5, ESV).

While recognizing Mary's important role, Protestants believe that intercession and devotion should be directed to Christ alone.

Areas of Agreement

Despite these differences, there are several areas of agreement between Protestant and Catholic views on Mary.

The Virgin Birth

Protestants universally affirm the doctrine of the virgin birth, based on biblical texts such as Matthew 1:18-25 and Luke 1:26-38. This belief is fundamental to the understanding of Jesus' divine nature.

Mary as Theotokos

Most Protestant traditions accept the title Theotokos (Mother of God) for Mary, acknowledging her role in bearing the incarnate Son of God. This title was affirmed by the Council of Ephesus in 431 AD and is seen as doctrinally sound within the context of Christ's divinity.

Mary's Role in the Incarnation

Protestants recognize and honor Mary's unique role in the Incarnation, seeing her as a model of faith and obedience. Her acceptance of God's will and her response to the angel Gabriel are seen as exemplary:

"And Mary said, 'Behold, I am the servant of the Lord; let it be to me according to your word.' And the angel departed from her" (Luke 1:38, ESV).

Strong's Exhaustive Concordance Analysis

Using Strong's Exhaustive Concordance, we can explore key biblical terms related to Protestant views on Mary:

- "Virgin" (Greek: παρθένος, parthenos): This term is used in the Annunciation narrative (Luke 1:27) to describe Mary, emphasizing her purity and the miraculous nature of Jesus' conception.

- "Mother of Jesus" (Greek: μήτηρ Ἰησοῦ, mētēr Iēsou): Used in the Gospels to denote Mary's maternal role, highlighting her relationship with Jesus (e.g., John 2:1-5).

Comprehensive Commentary Insights

Comprehensive commentaries provide deeper insights into Protestant interpretations of Mary:

- The New Jerome Biblical Commentary: This commentary explores the biblical foundations of Marian beliefs and how they have been interpreted differently across Christian traditions.

- The Anchor Yale Bible Commentary: It offers detailed analysis of biblical texts related to Mary and discusses Protestant perspectives on these texts.

Protestant Reflections on Mary

Mary as a Model of Faith

Protestants honor Mary as a model of faith and obedience. Her acceptance of God's plan and her role in the Incarnation are seen as exemplary for all believers:

"Blessed is she who believed that there would be a fulfillment of what was spoken to her from the Lord" (Luke 1:45, ESV).

Mary's Humility and Servanthood

Mary's humility and servanthood are emphasized in Protestant reflections, seeing her as a humble servant who responded faithfully to God's call:

"My soul magnifies the Lord, and my spirit rejoices in God my Savior, for he has looked on the humble estate of his servant" (Luke 1:46-48, ESV).

The Importance of Scripture

Protestants emphasize the importance of Scripture in understanding Mary's role. They focus on biblical texts and are cautious about doctrines and practices not explicitly supported by the Bible.

Conclusion: Mary in Protestant Theology

The Protestant perspective on Mary highlights both areas of agreement and significant theological differences with Catholic views. While rejecting certain doctrines such as the Immaculate Conception and the Assumption, Protestants honor Mary's unique role in the Incarnation and see her as a model of faith and obedience.

By examining the biblical foundations for these views, supported by exhaustive concordance analysis and comprehensive commentary, we gain a deeper understanding of the Protestant approach to Marian theology. This perspective emphasizes the importance of Scripture, the sole mediatorship of Christ, and the universal need for redemption.

Through this exploration, we see how Mary's role is honored and understood within Protestant theology, reflecting a commitment to biblical fidelity and a focus on the centrality of Christ in the life of faith.

CHAPTER 14

MARY AND INTERCESSORY PRAYER

The question of whether Mary can pray for us, and the broader concept of Marian intercession, has been a significant aspect of Catholic theology. This chapter will explore the biblical and theological basis for Marian intercession, examining relevant scriptural passages, supported by exhaustive concordance analysis and comprehensive commentary.

The Concept of Intercession in the Bible

Intercessory prayer, where one individual prays on behalf of another, is a well-established practice in both the Old and New Testaments.

Old Testament Examples

In the Old Testament, several figures intercede for others:

- Abraham: Abraham intercedes for Sodom and Gomorrah, pleading with God to spare the cities if righteous people can be found (Genesis 18:22-33).

- Moses: Moses frequently intercedes for the Israelites, asking God to forgive their sins and spare them from punishment (Exodus 32:11-14).

New Testament Examples

The New Testament also includes numerous examples of intercessory prayer:

- Jesus: Jesus intercedes for His disciples and future believers, as seen in His High Priestly Prayer (John 17:9, 20).

- The Apostles: The apostles pray for believers and for one another, highlighting the communal nature of intercession (Acts 12:5; Romans 1:9).

Mary's Role in Intercessory Prayer

Mary's role in intercession is rooted in her unique relationship with Jesus and her exemplary faith. The key biblical event that illustrates her intercessory role is the Wedding at Cana.

The Wedding at Cana: John 2:1-11

The Wedding at Cana is the first public miracle performed by Jesus, prompted by Mary's intercession:

"On the third day there was a wedding at Cana in Galilee, and the mother of Jesus was there. Jesus also was invited to the wedding with his disciples. When the wine ran out, the mother of Jesus said to him, 'They have no wine.' And Jesus said to her, 'Woman, what does this have to do with me? My hour has not yet come.' His mother said to the servants, 'Do whatever he tells you.' Now there were six stone water jars there for the Jewish rites of purification, each holding twenty or thirty gallons. Jesus said to the servants, 'Fill the jars with water.' And they filled them up to the brim. And he said to them, 'Now draw some out and take it to the master of the feast.' So they took it. When the master of the feast tasted the water now become wine, and did not know where it came from (though the servants who had drawn the water knew), the master of the feast called the bridegroom and said to him, 'Everyone serves the good wine first, and when people have drunk freely, then the poor wine. But you have kept the good wine until now.' This, the first of his signs, Jesus did at Cana in Galilee, and manifested his glory. And his disciples believed in him" (John 2:1-11, ESV).

Mary's intercession leads to Jesus' first miracle, highlighting her influential role in bringing requests to her son. This passage is often cited as a biblical basis for Marian intercession.

Strong's Exhaustive Concordance Analysis

- "Intercession" (Greek: ἔντευξις, enteuxis): While not used directly in reference to Mary, the concept of intercession (as seen in 1 Timothy 2:1) involves appealing on behalf of others, which Mary exemplifies at Cana.

Comprehensive Commentary Insights

- The New Jerome Biblical Commentary: This commentary highlights Mary's role at Cana as indicative of her intercessory power, showing her ability to bring needs to Jesus.

- The Anchor Yale Bible Commentary: It discusses the theological significance of Mary's intercession at Cana, noting its implications for her ongoing role in the Church.

Theological Basis for Marian Intercession

Catholic theology holds that Mary's intercessory role continues beyond her earthly life, based on her unique relationship with Jesus and her assumption into heaven.

The Communion of Saints

The doctrine of the Communion of Saints teaches that the saints in heaven can intercede for those on earth. This belief is rooted in the understanding that death does not sever the bonds of Christian fellowship.

- Hebrews 12:1: "Therefore, since we are surrounded by so great a cloud of witnesses, let us also lay aside every weight, and sin which clings so closely, and let us run with endurance the race that is set before us" (ESV).

This "cloud of witnesses" is understood to include Mary, who, as the mother of Jesus, holds a special place among the saints.

Mary's Assumption and Queenship

The doctrine of the Assumption, which teaches that Mary was taken body and soul into heavenly glory, supports the belief in her intercessory role. As Queen of Heaven, Mary is believed to have a special ability to intercede for believers.

- Revelation 12:1: "And a great sign appeared in heaven: a woman clothed with the sun, with the moon under her feet, and on her head a crown of twelve stars" (ESV).

This passage is often interpreted as symbolizing Mary's exaltation and her role as intercessor.

Prayers to Mary

Catholic prayers to Mary, such as the Hail Mary and the Rosary, reflect the belief in her intercessory power.

The Hail Mary

The Hail Mary is a prayer that combines Gabriel's greeting to Mary at the Annunciation with Elizabeth's greeting during the Visitation, followed by a petition for Mary's intercession:

"Hail Mary, full of grace, the Lord is with thee. Blessed art thou among women, and blessed is the fruit of thy womb, Jesus. Holy Mary, Mother of God, pray for us sinners, now and at the hour of our death. Amen."

The Rosary

The Rosary is a devotional prayer that involves meditating on key events in the lives of Jesus and Mary, known as the Mysteries. Each decade of the Rosary includes the Hail Mary, reflecting a continual petition for Mary's intercession.

Objections and Protestant Perspectives

Protestants generally reject the practice of praying to Mary and the saints, emphasizing the sole mediatorship of Christ:

- 1 Timothy 2:5: "For there is one God, and there is one mediator between God and men, the man Christ Jesus" (ESV).

Protestants argue that all prayers should be directed to God through Jesus Christ, who is the only mediator. They caution against practices that might detract from Christ's unique role.

Strong's Exhaustive Concordance Analysis

- "Mediator" (Greek: μεσίτης, mesitēs): This term, used in 1 Timothy 2:5, underscores Christ's unique role as the mediator between God and humanity.

Comprehensive Commentary Insights

- The New Jerome Biblical Commentary: This commentary explores the theological basis for Marian intercession and addresses common objections, emphasizing the distinction between Christ's unique mediatorship and the intercessory role of the saints.

- The Anchor Yale Bible Commentary: It provides a nuanced discussion on the practice of Marian intercession, acknowledging different Christian perspectives while highlighting the biblical and historical foundations for the Catholic view.

Conclusion: Mary and Intercessory Prayer

The Catholic belief in Marian intercession is rooted in Scripture and tradition, emphasizing Mary's unique relationship with Jesus and her ongoing role in the Communion of Saints. Biblical passages such as the Wedding at Cana and the vision in Revelation, supported by exhaustive concordance analysis and comprehensive commentary, provide a foundation for understanding Mary's intercessory power.

While Protestant perspectives generally reject the practice of praying to Mary, focusing instead on the sole mediatorship of Christ, the Catholic tradition honors Mary's role as a powerful intercessor who brings the needs of believers to her son.

By exploring the biblical and theological basis for Marian intercession, we gain a deeper appreciation for the nuances of this doctrine and its significance in the life of the Church. Mary's example of faith, humility, and maternal care continues to inspire and guide believers, reflecting her enduring legacy as a model of intercessory prayer.

CHAPTER 15

BRINGING THE DIVIDE: A BALANCED PERSPECTIVE ON MARY

The figure of Mary, the mother of Jesus, has often been a point of contention between Catholic and Protestant traditions. This chapter aims to propose a balanced perspective on Mary that respects her Jewish roots, honors her role in salvation history, and seeks to bridge the theological divide. By examining verified details and biblical evidence, supported by exhaustive concordance analysis and comprehensive commentary, we can find common ground and a fuller appreciation of Mary's significance.

Mary's Jewish Roots

Understanding Mary within her Jewish context is essential for appreciating her role in salvation history. Mary was a Jewish woman living in first-century Palestine, and her faith and actions were deeply rooted in Jewish tradition.

Mary in the Hebrew Scriptures

The Hebrew Scriptures provide a backdrop for Mary's life and mission. Several Old Testament figures and symbols foreshadow Mary's role:

- Eve: Mary is often seen as the New Eve, whose obedience contrasts with Eve's disobedience. The promise in Genesis 3:15 ("I will put enmity between you and the woman, and between your offspring and her offspring; he shall bruise your head, and you shall bruise his heel") is seen as a proto-evangelium, hinting at Mary's role in bearing the Messiah.

- Ark of the Covenant: Mary is likened to the Ark of the Covenant, which bore the presence of God. Just as the Ark carried the tablets of the Law, Aaron's rod, and manna, Mary bore Jesus, the Word made flesh (Exodus 25:10-22; Luke 1:35, 42-43).

Strong's Exhaustive Concordance Analysis

- "Woman" (Hebrew: אִשָּׁה, 'iššâ): The term used in Genesis 3:15 can be seen as a prophetic reference to Mary, highlighting her role in the battle against evil.

Mary's Role in Salvation History

Mary's role in salvation history is central to understanding her significance. Her participation in God's redemptive plan is highlighted in several key New Testament passages.

The Annunciation: Luke 1:26-38

The Annunciation narrative underscores Mary's unique role in the Incarnation:

"And the angel said to her, 'Do not be afraid, Mary, for you have found favor with God. And behold, you will conceive in your womb and bear a son, and you shall call his name Jesus. He will be great and will be called the Son of the Most High. And the Lord God will give to him the throne of his father David, and he will reign over the house of Jacob forever, and of his kingdom there will be no end'" (Luke 1:30-33, ESV).

Mary's acceptance of God's will, expressed in her fiat ("Behold, I am the servant of the Lord; let it be to me according to your word," Luke 1:38), highlights her faith and obedience.

The Magnificat: Luke 1:46-55

Mary's Magnificat reflects her deep faith and understanding of God's redemptive work:

"My soul magnifies the Lord, and my spirit rejoices in God my Savior, for he has looked on the humble estate of his servant. For behold, from now on all generations will call me blessed; for he who is mighty has done great things for me, and holy is his name" (Luke 1:46-49, ESV).

This hymn of praise reveals Mary's recognition of her role in God's plan and her gratitude for His mercy and faithfulness.

Bridging the Catholic and Protestant Divide

A balanced perspective on Mary seeks to honor her role while addressing theological differences between Catholic and Protestant views.

Catholic Perspective

The Catholic Church venerates Mary and upholds several key doctrines, such as the Immaculate Conception, the Assumption, and her role as intercessor. These doctrines are rooted in a long tradition of theological reflection and devotion.

- Immaculate Conception: The belief that Mary was conceived without original sin (Ineffabilis Deus, 1854).

- Assumption: The belief that Mary was taken body and soul into heaven at the end of her earthly life (Munificentissimus Deus, 1950).

- Intercession: The practice of seeking Mary's intercession, as exemplified in prayers like the Hail Mary and the Rosary.

Protestant Perspective

Protestants generally honor Mary as the mother of Jesus but reject certain Catholic doctrines and practices, emphasizing scriptural foundations and the sole mediatorship of Christ.

- Virgin Birth: Universally accepted, based on biblical texts such as Matthew 1:18-25 and Luke 1:26-38.

- Mary as Theotokos: Accepted as the Mother of God, acknowledging her role in bearing the incarnate Son of God.

- Intercession: Rejected, with a focus on Christ as the sole mediator (1 Timothy 2:5).

Finding Common Ground

Honoring Mary's Role

Both traditions can agree on the importance of honoring Mary's role in the Incarnation and her exemplary faith. Recognizing her unique contribution to salvation history provides a foundation for mutual respect and dialogue.

Emphasizing Biblical Foundations

Focusing on the biblical foundations for Marian beliefs allows for a shared understanding of her significance.

Key passages, such as the Annunciation and the Magnificat, highlight her faith and obedience, which can be appreciated by both traditions.

Respecting Theological Differences

Acknowledging and respecting theological differences is crucial for fostering dialogue. While Catholics may uphold doctrines like the Immaculate Conception and the Assumption, Protestants can appreciate Mary's role without endorsing these specific beliefs.

Exploring Mary's Jewish Roots

Emphasizing Mary's Jewish roots and her place within the broader narrative of God's covenant with Israel provides a common ground for understanding her significance. Recognizing Mary's heritage enriches our appreciation of her role and fosters a deeper connection to the shared biblical tradition.

Strong's Exhaustive Concordance Analysis

- "Blessed" (Greek: εὐλογημένη, eulogēmenē): Used in Luke 1:42, this term highlights Mary's blessedness among women, reflecting her honored status.

- "Grace" (Greek: χάρις, charis): Used in Luke 1:28 ("full of grace"), indicating the unique divine favor bestowed upon Mary.

Comprehensive Commentary Insights

- The New Jerome Biblical Commentary: This commentary explores the theological significance of Mary's role in the New Testament and its development in Christian tradition.

- The Anchor Yale Bible Commentary: It provides a detailed analysis of biblical texts related to Mary and discusses their implications for both Catholic and Protestant theology.

Conclusion: A Balanced Perspective on Mary

A balanced perspective on Mary respects her Jewish roots, honors her role in salvation history, and seeks to bridge the divide between Catholic and Protestant views. By focusing on shared biblical foundations and recognizing theological differences, we can foster mutual respect and appreciation for Mary's significance.

Mary's example of faith, humility, and obedience continues to inspire and guide believers. Whether viewed through a Catholic or Protestant lens, her unique role in God's redemptive plan remains a central and unifying aspect of Christian faith. Through dialogue and understanding, we can celebrate Mary's legacy and draw closer to a fuller, richer appreciation of her place in the story of salvation.

CHAPTER 16

EMBRACING THE FULLNESS OF MARY'S LEGACY

As we conclude this exploration of Mary's legacy, it is essential to reflect on the key points discussed throughout this book and encourage a fuller understanding of her significance in the Christian faith. By examining Mary's Jewish roots, her role in salvation history, and the diverse perspectives within Catholic and Protestant traditions, we gain a deeper appreciation of her place in God's redemptive plan. This conclusion will summarize these insights and emphasize the importance of embracing the richness of Mary's legacy.

Mary's Jewish Roots and Biblical Foreshadowing

Understanding Mary's Jewish heritage is foundational to appreciating her role. Mary's life and actions are deeply rooted in the traditions and prophecies of the Hebrew Scriptures.

Key Biblical References

- Genesis 3:15: The proto-evangelium foreshadows Mary's role in salvation, highlighting her as the "woman" whose offspring would defeat the serpent.

- Isaiah 7:14: The prophecy of the virgin birth, fulfilled in Mary's conception of Jesus, underscores her pivotal role in God's plan.

- Exodus 25:10-22: The Ark of the Covenant, which bore the presence of God, prefigures Mary as the new Ark, bearing Jesus, the Word made flesh.

Mary's Role in Salvation History

Mary's role in salvation history is central to Christian theology. Her faith, obedience, and participation in the Incarnation highlight her unique contribution to God's redemptive work.

Key New Testament Passages

- Luke 1:26-38: The Annunciation narrative emphasizes Mary's acceptance of God's will, marking the beginning of the Incarnation.

- Luke 1:46-55: The Magnificat reflects Mary's profound faith and understanding of God's redemptive plan.

- John 2:1-11: The Wedding at Cana illustrates Mary's intercessory role and her influence in Jesus' public ministry.

Doctrinal Developments in Catholic Theology

Catholic theology has developed several key doctrines to honor Mary's unique role, reflecting deep theological reflection and devotion.

Key Doctrines

- Immaculate Conception: The belief that Mary was conceived without original sin, emphasizing her purity and sanctity (Ineffabilis Deus, 1854).

- Assumption: The belief that Mary was taken body and soul into heavenly glory, affirming her exalted status (Munificentissimus Deus, 1950).

- Intercession: The practice of seeking Mary's intercession, rooted in her unique relationship with Jesus and her role in the Communion of Saints.

Protestant Perspectives on Mary

Protestant theology honors Mary's role in the Incarnation while emphasizing scriptural foundations and the sole mediatorship of Christ.

Key Views

- Virgin Birth: Universally affirmed, based on biblical texts such as Matthew 1:18-25 and Luke 1:26-38.

- Mary as Theotokos: Accepted as the Mother of God, acknowledging her role in bearing the incarnate Son of God.

- Focus on Christ: Emphasizing Christ's unique mediatorship, with intercession directed solely to Him (1 Timothy 2:5).

Bridging the Divide

A balanced perspective on Mary seeks to honor her role while addressing theological differences between Catholic and Protestant views. Focusing on shared biblical foundations and respecting theological differences fosters mutual understanding and appreciation.

Common Ground

- Honoring Mary's Role: Both traditions can agree on the importance of honoring Mary's role in the Incarnation and her exemplary faith.

- Biblical Foundations: Emphasizing the biblical foundations for Marian beliefs allows for a shared understanding of her significance.

- Respecting Differences: Acknowledging and respecting theological differences is crucial for fostering dialogue and unity.

Strong's Exhaustive Concordance Analysis

- "Blessed" (Greek: εὐλογημένη, eulogēmenē): Used in Luke 1:42, highlighting Mary's blessedness among women.

- "Grace" (Greek: χάρις, charis): Used in Luke 1:28 ("full of grace"), indicating the unique divine favor bestowed upon Mary.

Comprehensive Commentary Insights

- The New Jerome Biblical Commentary: Explores the theological significance of Mary's role in the New Testament and its development in Christian tradition.

- The Anchor Yale Bible Commentary: Provides detailed analysis of biblical texts related to Mary and discusses their implications for both Catholic and Protestant theology.

Embracing Mary's Legacy

Mary's legacy is rich and multifaceted, encompassing her role as the Mother of God, the New Eve, the Queen of Heaven, and a powerful intercessor. By embracing the fullness of her legacy, we honor her unique contribution to salvation history and deepen our understanding of her significance in the Christian faith.

Practical Steps

- Study and Reflection: Engage in personal and communal study of the biblical texts and theological writings related to Mary.

- Prayer and Devotion: Incorporate prayers and devotions that honor Mary's role and seek her intercession, while maintaining a Christ-centered focus.

- Dialogue and Unity: Foster respectful dialogue between Catholic and Protestant traditions, seeking common ground and appreciating theological differences.

Conclusion

Mary's legacy is a testament to her profound faith, humility, and obedience. As the Mother of Jesus, she played an indispensable role in God's redemptive plan. By exploring her Jewish roots, her role in salvation history, and the diverse perspectives within Catholic and Protestant traditions, we gain a fuller appreciation of her significance.

Embracing Mary's legacy enriches our faith and deepens our connection to the broader Christian tradition. Through study, prayer, and dialogue, we can honor her unique role and draw closer to the heart of the Gospel message. Mary's example continues to inspire and guide believers, reflecting her enduring legacy as a model of faith and devotion.

APPENDICES

Appendix A: Key Biblical Passages Related to Mary

This appendix lists and provides brief explanations of the key biblical passages related to Mary, highlighting their significance in Marian theology.

Genesis 3:15

"And I will put enmity between you and the woman, and between your offspring and her offspring; he shall bruise your head, and you shall bruise his heel."

This verse is often referred to as the proto-evangelium, or "first gospel," foreshadowing Mary's role in salvation history as the mother of the Messiah.

Isaiah 7:14

"Therefore the Lord himself will give you a sign. Behold, the virgin shall conceive and bear a son, and shall call his name Immanuel."

This prophecy is seen as a direct reference to the virgin birth of Jesus, highlighting Mary's role in the Incarnation.

Luke 1:26-38 (The Annunciation)

"In the sixth month the angel Gabriel was sent from God to a city of Galilee named Nazareth, to a virgin betrothed to a man whose name was Joseph, of the house of David. And the virgin's name was Mary..."

This passage describes the angel Gabriel's announcement to Mary that she would conceive and bear the Son of God, emphasizing her obedience and faith.

Luke 1:39-45 (The Visitation)

"In those days Mary arose and went with haste into the hill country, to a town in Judah, and she entered the house of Zechariah and greeted Elizabeth..."

Mary visits her cousin Elizabeth, who acknowledges Mary's blessedness and the significance of her role.

Luke 1:46-55 (The Magnificat)

"And Mary said, 'My soul magnifies the Lord, and my spirit rejoices in God my Savior...'"

Mary's song of praise reflects her deep faith and recognition of God's mercy and power.

Matthew 1:18-25 (The Birth of Jesus)

"Now the birth of Jesus Christ took place in this way. When his mother Mary had been betrothed to Joseph, before they came together she was found to be with child from the Holy Spirit..."

This passage details the events surrounding the birth of Jesus, highlighting the miraculous nature of His conception.

John 2:1-11 (The Wedding at Cana)

"On the third day there was a wedding at Cana in Galilee, and the mother of Jesus was there..."

Mary's intercession at the wedding leads to Jesus performing His first miracle, turning water into wine.

John 19:25-27 (At the Cross)

"But standing by the cross of Jesus were his mother and his mother's sister, Mary the wife of Clopas, and Mary Magdalene..."

Jesus entrusts Mary to the care of the beloved disciple, highlighting her role within the Christian community.

Revelation 12:1-6

"And a great sign appeared in heaven: a woman clothed with the sun, with the moon under her feet, and on her head a crown of twelve stars..."

This passage is often interpreted as symbolizing Mary, reflecting her exaltation and ongoing role in the Church.

Appendix B: Marian Doctrines and Dogmas

This appendix provides an overview of key Marian doctrines and dogmas, including their definitions and historical developments.

The Immaculate Conception

- Definition: The doctrine that Mary was conceived without original sin.

- Declared: December 8, 1854, by Pope Pius IX in the apostolic constitution "Ineffabilis Deus."

- Significance: Emphasizes Mary's purity and her unique role in salvation history.

The Assumption

- Definition: The doctrine that Mary was taken body and soul into heavenly glory at the end of her earthly life.

- Declared: November 1, 1950, by Pope Pius XII in the apostolic constitution "Munificentissimus Deus."

- Significance: Highlights Mary's exalted status and her participation in the resurrection.

Mary as Theotokos (Mother of God)

- Definition: The title affirming Mary as the mother of Jesus, who is both fully God and fully human.

- Declared: Council of Ephesus, 431 AD.

- Significance: Confirms the unity of Jesus' divine and human natures.

Perpetual Virginity

- Definition: The belief that Mary remained a virgin before, during, and after the birth of Jesus.

- Historical Support: Affirmed by early Church Fathers and ecumenical councils.

- Significance: Emphasizes Mary's special role and her dedication to God.

Mary as Intercessor

- Definition: The belief that Mary intercedes for believers, bringing their petitions to her son, Jesus.

- Biblical Basis: Illustrated by Mary's intercession at the Wedding at Cana (John 2:1-11).

- Significance: Reflects Mary's maternal care and her ongoing role in the Church.

Appendix C: Key Marian Prayers and Devotions

This appendix lists and explains key Marian prayers and devotions practiced within the Catholic tradition.

Hail Mary

- Text: "Hail Mary, full of grace, the Lord is with thee. Blessed art thou among women, and blessed is the fruit of thy womb, Jesus. Holy Mary, Mother of God, pray for us sinners, now and at the hour of our death. Amen."

- Significance: Combines Gabriel's greeting (Luke 1:28) and Elizabeth's greeting (Luke 1:42) with a petition for Mary's intercession.

The Rosary

- Structure: A series of prayers, including the Our Father, Hail Mary, and Glory Be, meditated upon in five-decade cycles focusing on the Mysteries of Christ's life.

- Significance: Reflects on key events in the lives of Jesus and Mary, fostering deeper spiritual contemplation and connection.

The Magnificat

- Text: "My soul magnifies the Lord, and my spirit rejoices in God my Savior..." (Luke 1:46-55).

- Significance: Mary's song of praise, reflecting her deep faith and recognition of God's work in her life.

The Angelus

- Text: "The Angel of the Lord declared unto Mary, and she conceived of the Holy Spirit..." followed by the Hail Mary, repeated three times daily.

- Significance: Commemorates the Annunciation and honors Mary's role in the Incarnation.

Litany of the Blessed Virgin Mary (Litany of Loreto)

- Text: A series of invocations and responses honoring Mary under various titles and attributes.

- Significance: Highlights the various aspects of Mary's role and her virtues.

Appendix D: Key Figures in Marian Theology

This appendix provides brief biographies of key figures in the development of Marian theology.

St. Augustine of Hippo (354-430)

- Contributions: Emphasized Mary's perpetual virginity and her role as the Mother of God.

- Works: "On Holy Virginity," "Sermons."

St. Thomas Aquinas (1225-1274)

- Contributions: Provided theological foundations for Marian doctrines, including the Immaculate Conception.

- Works: "Summa Theologica."

St. Bernard of Clairvaux (1090-1153)

- Contributions: Promoted Marian devotion and wrote extensively on Mary's intercessory role.

- Works: "Sermons on the Song of Songs."

St. Louis de Montfort (1673-1716)

- Contributions: Advocated for total consecration to Mary and deepened Marian spirituality.

- Works: "True Devotion to Mary."

Pope Pius IX (1792-1878)

- Contributions: Declared the dogma of the Immaculate Conception.

- Works: "Ineffabilis Deus."

Pope Pius XII (1876-1958)

- Contributions: Declared the dogma of the Assumption.

- Works: "Munificentissimus Deus."

By including these appendices, readers gain a comprehensive understanding of the biblical, historical, and theological foundations of Marian beliefs and practices, enriching their appreciation of Mary's enduring legacy in the Christian faith.